A TOPICAL
LOOK AT
THE BOOK
OF ISAIAH

A TOPICAL LOOK AT THE BOOK OF ISAIAH

Compiled by Eugene Carvalho

A Topical Look at the Book of Isaiah

Copyright © 2010 by Eugene Carvalho

In the U.S. write:
Eugene Carvalho
500 Waterman Avenue
East Providence, RI 02914
Telephone: 401 215 3171
Facsimile: 401 438 1992
Web Site: www.newwinemissions.info

ISBN 10: 1461100550
ISBN 13: 978-1461100553

Printed in the United States of America

To the Body of Christ.
May this compilation bless you richly!
With love...

TABLE OF CONTENTS

PURPOSE & ACKNOWLEDGEMENTS

The infallible Word of God for faith and conduct informs us that the Holy Spirit gives gifts to men and women of the Body of Christ. It states: "the gifts edify the body for the building up of the saints" (Eph. 4:12). I hope the talents and gifts the Lord has given me will be a blessing to someone else through the reading of this compilation.

I am grateful for the love from all family members, especially my parents Mary and Eugenio Carvalho. I am also grateful for the knowledge, wisdom and love of many pastors, teachers, and saints that the Lord has used to bless me. Lastly, I must not forget a special thank you to my dear friend Kathryn Regan for proofreading this material.

Chapter One

LAYING A FOUNDATION

I must start off by giving the Lord a shout of praise for using me to write another Christian book for His glory. It is vital to understand clearly that a Christian must base everything they believe and lay a foundation solely on what is written in the Bible.

Our minds must be renewed day by day by God's precious Word. I want to introduce three sets of scriptures that will reinforce our vital need to study the Scriptures on a daily basis. The Bible says, "So faith comes from hearing, and hearing by the word of Christ" (Ro. 10:17).[1] "This book of the law shall not depart from your mouth, but you shall meditate on it day and night, so that you may be careful to do according to all that is written in it; for then you will make your way prosperous, and then you will have success" (Jos. 1:8). "…If you continue in My word, then you are truly disciples of Mine; and you will know the truth, and the truth will make you free" (Jn. 8:31-32).

Isaiah's prophetic ministry covers over forty years, spanning the reigns of four kings of Judah. Salvation is the central theme in the Book of Isaiah. A topical look will give you fresh insight and strengthen your Spirit tremendously!

Allow me at this time to inform you of three more sets of scriptures that inform us of the importance of studying God infallible Word. The Bible says, "Be diligent to present yourself approved to God as a workman who does not need to be ashamed, accurately handling the word of truth" (2 Tim. 2:15). "All Scripture is inspired by God and profitable for teaching, for reproof, for correction,

---

[1] From this point forward all Scripture quotations, unless otherwise noted, are from the *New American Standard Bible.*

for training in righteousness; so that the man of God may be adequate, equipped for every good work" (2 Tim. 3:16-17). "Preach the word; be ready in season and out of season; reprove, rebuke, exhort, with great patience and instruction" (2 Tim. 4:2).

I suggest you let the Holy Spirit put these scriptures deep inside your Spirit. Do not rush. Each day take one topic and meditate on all of those scriptures. Also, I included a topic index in the back of the book for your convenience.

Chapter Two

A TOPICAL LOOK

ABOMINATION
Isa. 1:13 - Bring your worthless offerings no longer, Incense is an abomination to Me. New moon and sabbath, the calling of assemblies— I cannot endure iniquity and the solemn assembly.

Isa. 41:24 - Behold, you are of no account, And your work amounts to nothing; He who chooses you is an abomination.

Isa. 44:19 - No one recalls, nor is there knowledge or understanding to say, "I have burned half of it in the fire and also have baked bread over its coals. I roast meat and eat it. Then I make the rest of it into an abomination, I fall down before a block of wood!"

ABUNDANCE
Isa. 7:22 - And because of the abundance of the milk produced he will eat curds, for everyone that is left within the land will eat curds and honey.

Isa. 15:7 - Therefore the abundance which they have acquired and stored up They carry off over the brook of Arabim.

Isa. 55:2 - Why do you spend money for what is not bread, And your wages for what does not satisfy? Listen carefully to Me, and eat what is good, And delight yourself in abundance.

Isa. 60:5 - Then you will see and be radiant, And your heart will thrill and rejoice; Because the abundance of the sea will be turned to you, The wealth of the nations will come to you.

Isa. 63:7 - I shall make mention of the lovingkindnesses of the Lord, the praises of the Lord, According to all that the Lord has granted us, And the great goodness toward the house of Israel, Which He has granted them according to His compassion And according to the abundance of His lovingkindnesses.

AFFLICTED

Isa. 11:4 - But with righteousness He will judge the poor, And decide with fairness for the afflicted of the earth; And He will strike the earth with the rod of His mouth, And with the breath of His lips He will slay the wicked.

Isa. 14:32 - How then will one answer the messengers of the nation? That the Lord has founded Zion, And the afflicted of His people will seek refuge in it.

Isa. 21:10 - O my threshed people, and my afflicted of the threshing floor! What I have heard from the Lord of hosts, The God of Israel, I make known to you.

Isa. 26:6 - The foot will trample it, The feet of the afflicted, the steps of the helpless.

Isa. 29:19 - The afflicted also will increase their gladness in the Lord, And the needy of mankind will rejoice in the Holy One of Israel.

Isa. 32:7 - As for a rogue, his weapons are evil; He devises wicked schemes To destroy the afflicted with slander, Even though the needy one speaks what is right.

Isa. 41:17 - The afflicted and needy are seeking water, but there is none, And their tongue is parched with thirst; I, the Lord, will answer them Myself, As the God of Israel I will not forsake them.

Isa. 49:13 - Shout for joy, O heavens! And rejoice, O earth! Break forth into joyful shouting, O mountains! For the Lord has comforted His people And will have compassion on His afflicted.

Isa. 51:21 - Therefore, please hear this, you afflicted, Who are drunk, but not with wine.

Isa. 53:4 - Surely our griefs He Himself bore, And our sorrows He carried; Yet we ourselves esteemed Him stricken, Smitten of God, and afflicted.

Isa. 53:7 - He was oppressed and He was afflicted, Yet He did not open His mouth; Like a lamb that is led to slaughter, And like a sheep that is silent before its shearers, So He did not open His mouth.

Isa. 54:11 - O afflicted one, storm-tossed, and not comforted, Behold, I will set your stones in antimony, And your foundations I will lay in sapphires.

Isa. 58:10 - And if you give yourself to the hungry And satisfy the desire of the afflicted, Then your light will rise in darkness And your gloom will become like midday.

Isa. 60:14 - The sons of those who afflicted you will come bowing to you, And all those who despised you will bow themselves at the soles of your feet; And they will call you the city of the Lord, The Zion of the Holy One of Israel.

Isa. 61:1 - The Spirit of the Lord God is upon me, Because the Lord has anointed me To bring good news to the afflicted; He has sent me to bind up the brokenhearted, To proclaim liberty to captives And freedom to prisoners.

Isa. 63:9 - In all their affliction He was afflicted, And the angel of His presence saved them; In His love and in His mercy He redeemed them, And He lifted them and carried them all the days of old.

ANGER

Isa. 5:25 - On this account the anger of the Lord has burned against His people, And He has stretched out His hand against them and struck them down. And the mountains quaked, and their corpses lay like refuse in the middle of the streets. For all this His anger is not spent, But His hand is still stretched out.

Isa. 7:4 - And say to him, 'Take care and be calm, have no fear and do not be fainthearted because of these two stubs of smoldering firebrands, on account of the fierce anger of Rezin and Aram and the son of Remaliah.

Isa. 9:12 - The Arameans on the east and the Philistines on the west; And they devour Israel with gaping jaws. In spite of all this, His anger does not turn away And His hand is still stretched out.

Isa. 9:17 - Therefore the Lord does not take pleasure in their young men, Nor does He have pity on their orphans or their widows; For every one of them is godless and an evildoer, And every mouth is speaking foolishness. In spite of all this, His anger does not turn away And His hand is still stretched out.

Isa. 9:21 - Manasseh devours Ephraim, and Ephraim Manasseh, And together they are against Judah. In spite of all this, His anger does not turn away And His hand is still stretched out.

Isa. 10:4 - Nothing remains but to crouch among the captives Or fall among the slain. In spite of all this, His anger does not turn away And His hand is still stretched out.

Isa. 10:5 - Woe to Assyria, the rod of My anger And the staff in whose hands is My indignation.

Isa. 10:25 - For in a very little while My indignation against you will be spent and My anger will be directed to their destruction.

Isa. 12:1 - Then you will say on that day, "I will give thanks to You, O Lord; For although You were angry with me, Your anger is turned away, And You comfort me."

Isa. 13:3 - I have commanded My consecrated ones, I have even called My mighty warriors, My proudly exulting ones, To execute My anger.

Isa. 13:9 - Behold, the day of the Lord is coming, Cruel, with fury and burning anger, To make the land a desolation; And He will exterminate its sinners from it.

Isa. 13:13 - Therefore I will make the heavens tremble, And the earth will be shaken from its place At the fury of the Lord of hosts In the day of His burning anger.

Isa. 14:6 - Which used to strike the peoples in fury with unceasing strokes, Which subdued the nations in anger with unrestrained persecution.

Isa. 30:27 - Behold, the name of the Lord comes from a remote place; Burning is His anger and dense is His smoke; His lips are filled with indignation And His tongue is like a consuming fire.

Isa. 30:30 - And the Lord will cause His voice of authority to be heard, And the descending of His arm to be seen in fierce anger, And in the flame of a consuming fire In cloudburst, downpour and hailstones.

Isa. 42:25 - So He poured out on him the heat of His anger And the fierceness of battle; And it set him aflame all around, Yet he did not recognize it; And it burned him, but he paid no attention.

Isa. 51:17 - Rouse yourself! Rouse yourself! Arise, O Jerusalem, You who have drunk from the Lord's hand the cup of His anger; The chalice of reeling you have drained to the dregs.

Isa. 51:22 - Thus says your Lord, the Lord, even your God Who contends for His people, "Behold, I have taken out of your hand the cup of reeling, The chalice of My anger; You will never drink it again."

Isa. 54:8 – "In an outburst of anger I hid My face from you for a moment, But with everlasting lovingkindness

I will have compassion on you," Says the Lord your Redeemer.

Isa. 63:3 - I have trodden the wine trough alone, And from the peoples there was no man with Me. I also trod them in My anger And trampled them in My wrath; And their lifeblood is sprinkled on My garments, And I stained all My raiment.

Isa. 63:6 - I trod down the peoples in My anger And made them drunk in My wrath, And I poured out their lifeblood on the earth.

Isa. 66:15 - For behold, the Lord will come in fire And His chariots like the whirlwind, To render His anger with fury, And His rebuke with flames of fire.

ANOINTED

Isa. 45:1 - Thus says the Lord to Cyrus His anointed, Whom I have taken by the right hand, To subdue nations before him And to loose the loins of kings; To open doors before him so that gates will not be shut.

Isa. 61:1 - The Spirit of the Lord God is upon me, Because the Lord has anointed me To bring good news to the afflicted; He has sent me to bind up the brokenhearted, To proclaim liberty to captives And freedom to prisoners.

ASTRAY

Isa. 3:12 - O My people! Their oppressors are children, And women rule over them. O My people! Those who guide you lead you astray And confuse the direction of your paths.

Isa. 9:16 - For those who guide this people are leading them astray; And those who are guided by them are brought to confusion.

Isa. 19:13 - The princes of Zoan have acted foolishly, The princes of Memphis are deluded; Those who are the cornerstone of her tribes Have led Egypt astray.

Isa. 19:14 - The Lord has mixed within her a spirit of distortion; They have led Egypt astray in all that it does, As a drunken man staggers in his vomit.

Isa. 53:6 - All of us like sheep have gone astray, Each of us has turned to his own way; But the Lord has caused the iniquity of us all To fall on Him.

ATTENTION

Isa. 5:12 - Their banquets are accompanied by lyre and harp, by tambourine and flute, and by wine; But they do not pay attention to the deeds of the Lord, Nor do they consider the work of His hands.

Isa. 10:30 - Cry aloud with your voice, O daughter of Gallim! Pay attention, Laishah and wretched Anathoth!

Isa. 21:7 - When he sees riders, horsemen in pairs, A train of donkeys, a train of camels, Let him pay close attention, very close attention.

Isa. 42:25 - So He poured out on him the heat of His anger And the fierceness of battle; And it set him aflame all around, Yet he did not recognize it; And it burned him, but he paid no attention.

Isa. 48:18 - If only you had paid attention to My commandments! Then your well-being would have been like a river, And your righteousness like the waves of the sea.

Isa. 49:1 - Listen to Me, O islands, And pay attention, you peoples from afar. The Lord called Me from the womb; From the body of My mother He named Me.

Isa. 51:4 - Pay attention to Me, O My people, And give ear to Me, O My nation; For a law will go forth from Me, And I will set My justice for a light of the peoples.

AWAKE

Isa. 26:19 - Your dead will live; Their corpses will rise. You who lie in the dust, awake and shout for joy, For your dew is as the dew of the dawn, And the earth will give birth to the departed spirits.

Isa. 51:9 - Awake, awake, put on strength, O arm of the Lord; Awake as in the days of old, the generations of long ago. Was it not You who cut Rahab in pieces, Who pierced the dragon?

Isa. 52:1 - Awake, awake, Clothe yourself in your strength, O Zion; Clothe yourself in your beautiful garments, O Jerusalem, the holy city; For the uncircumcised and the unclean Will no longer come into you.

BAREFOOT

Isa. 20:2 - At that time the Lord spoke through Isaiah the son of Amoz, saying, "Go and loosen the sackcloth from your hips and take your shoes off your feet." And he did so, going naked and barefoot.

Isa. 20:3 - And the Lord said, "Even as My servant Isaiah has gone naked and barefoot three years as a sign and token against Egypt and Cush."

Isa. 20:4 - So the king of Assyria will lead away the captives of Egypt and the exiles of Cush, young and old, naked and barefoot with buttocks uncovered, to the shame of Egypt.

BATTLE

Isa. 3:25 - Your men will fall by the sword And your mighty ones in battle.

Isa. 9:4 - For You shall break the yoke of their burden and the staff on their shoulders, The rod of their oppressor, as at the battle of Midian.

Isa. 9:5 - For every boot of the booted warrior in the battle tumult, And cloak rolled in blood, will be for burning, fuel for the fire.

Isa. 13:4 - A sound of tumult on the mountains, Like that of many people! A sound of the uproar of kingdoms, Of nations gathered together! The Lord of hosts is mustering the army for battle.

Isa. 21:15 - For they have fled from the swords, From the drawn sword, and from the bent bow And from the press of battle.

Isa. 22:2 - You who were full of noise, You boisterous town, you exultant city; Your slain were not slain with the sword, Nor did they die in battle.

Isa. 27:4 - I have no wrath. Should someone give Me briars and thorns in battle, Then I would step on them, I would burn them completely.

Isa. 29:3 - I will camp against you encircling you, And I will set siegeworks against you, And I will raise up battle towers against you.

Isa. 42:25 - So He poured out on him the heat of His anger And the fierceness of battle; And it set him aflame all around, Yet he did not recognize it; And it burned him, but he paid no attention.

BEASTS

Isa. 18:6 - They will be left together for mountain birds of prey, And for the beasts of the earth; And the birds of prey will spend the summer feeding on them, And all the beasts of the earth will spend harvest time on them.

Isa. 30:6 - The oracle concerning the beasts of the Negev. Through a land of distress and anguish, From where come lioness and lion, viper and flying serpent, They carry their riches on the backs of young donkeys

And their treasures on camels' humps, To a people who cannot profit them.

Isa. 40:16 - Even Lebanon is not enough to burn, Nor its beasts enough for a burnt offering.

Isa. 43:20 - The beasts of the field will glorify Me, The jackals and the ostriches, Because I have given waters in the wilderness And rivers in the desert, To give drink to My chosen people.

Isa. 46:1 - Bel has bowed down, Nebo stoops over; Their images are consigned to the beasts and the cattle. The things that you carry are burdensome, A load for the weary beast.

Isa. 56:9 - All you beasts of the field, All you beasts in the forest, Come to eat.

BEAUTIFUL

Isa. 2:16 - Against all the ships of Tarshish And against all the beautiful craft.

Isa. 4:2 - In that day the Branch of the Lord will be beautiful and glorious, and the fruit of the earth will be the pride and the adornment of the survivors of Israel.

Isa. 28:5 - In that day the Lord of hosts will become a beautiful crown And a glorious diadem to the remnant of His people.

Isa. 52:1 - Awake, awake, Clothe yourself in your strength, O Zion; Clothe yourself in your beautiful garments, O Jerusalem, the holy city; For the uncircumcised and the unclean Will no longer come into you.

Isa. 64:11 - Our holy and beautiful house, Where our fathers praised You, Has been burned by fire; And all our precious things have become a ruin.

BRUISED
Isa. 42:3 - A bruised reed He will not break And a dimly burning wick He will not extinguish; He will faithfully bring forth justice.

BONDS
Isa. 58:6 - Is this not the fast which I choose, To loosen the bonds of wickedness, To undo the bands of the yoke, And to let the oppressed go free And break every yoke?

BORE
Isa. 53:4 - Surely our griefs He Himself bore, And our sorrows He carried; Yet we ourselves esteemed Him stricken, Smitten of God, and afflicted.
Isa. 53:12 - Therefore, I will allot Him a portion with the great, And He will divide the booty with the strong; Because He poured out Himself to death, And was numbered with the transgressors; Yet He Himself bore the sin of many, And interceded for the transgressors.

BRANCH
Isa. 4:2 - In that day the Branch of the Lord will be beautiful and glorious, and the fruit of the earth will be the pride and the adornment of the survivors of Israel.
Isa. 9:14 - So the Lord cuts off head and tail from Israel, Both palm branch and bulrush in a single day.
Isa. 11:1 - Then a shoot will spring from the stem of Jesse, And a branch from his roots will bear fruit.
Isa. 14:19 - But you have been cast out of your tomb Like a rejected branch, Clothed with the slain who are pierced with a sword, Who go down to the stones of the pit Like a trampled corpse.

Isa. 19:15 - There will be no work for Egypt Which its head or tail, its palm branch or bulrush, may do.

Isa. 60:21 - Then all your people will be righteous; They will possess the land forever, The branch of My planting, The work of My hands, That I may be glorified.

BRIDEGROOM

Isa. 61:10 - I will rejoice greatly in the Lord, My soul will exult in my God; For He has clothed me with garments of salvation, He has wrapped me with a robe of righteousness, As a bridegroom decks himself with a garland, And as a bride adorns herself with her jewels.

Isa. 62:5 - For as a young man marries a virgin, So your sons will marry you; And as the bridegroom rejoices over the bride, So your God will rejoice over you.

CHOSEN

Isa. 1:29 - Surely you will be ashamed of the oaks which you have desired, And you will be embarrassed at the gardens which you have chosen.

Isa. 41:8 - But you, Israel, My servant, Jacob whom I have chosen, Descendant of Abraham My friend.

Isa. 41:9 - You whom I have taken from the ends of the earth, And called from its remotest parts And said to you, 'You are My servant, I have chosen you and not rejected you.

Isa. 42:1 - Behold, My Servant, whom I uphold; My chosen one in whom My soul delights. I have put My Spirit upon Him; He will bring forth justice to the nations.

Isa. 43:10 – "You are My witnesses," declares the Lord, "And My servant whom I have chosen, So that you may know and believe Me And understand that I am

He. Before Me there was no God formed, And there will be none after Me."

Isa. 43:20 - The beasts of the field will glorify Me, The jackals and the ostriches, Because I have given waters in the wilderness And rivers in the desert, To give drink to My chosen people.

Isa. 44:1 - But now listen, O Jacob, My servant, And Israel, whom I have chosen.

Isa. 44:2 - Thus says the Lord who made you And formed you from the womb, who will help you, 'Do not fear, O Jacob My servant; And you Jeshurun whom I have chosen.

Isa. 45:4 - For the sake of Jacob My servant, And Israel My chosen one, I have also called you by your name; I have given you a title of honor Though you have not known Me.

Isa. 49:7 - Thus says the Lord, the Redeemer of Israel and its Holy One, To the despised One, To the One abhorred by the nation, To the Servant of rulers, "Kings will see and arise, Princes will also bow down, Because of the Lord who is faithful, the Holy One of Israel who has chosen You."

Isa. 65:9 - I will bring forth offspring from Jacob, And an heir of My mountains from Judah; Even My chosen ones shall inherit it, And My servants will dwell there.

Isa. 65:15 - You will leave your name for a curse to My chosen ones, And the Lord God will slay you. But My servants will be called by another name.

Isa. 65:22 - They will not build and another inhabit, They will not plant and another eat; For as the lifetime of a tree, so will be the days of My people, And My chosen ones will wear out the work of their hands.

Isa. 66:3 - But he who kills an ox is like one who slays a man; He who sacrifices a lamb is like the one who breaks a dog's neck; He who offers a grain offering is like one who offers swine's blood; He who burns incense is like the one who blesses an idol. As they have chosen their own ways, And their soul delights in their abominations.

CLOUD

Isa. 4:5 - Then the Lord will create over the whole area of Mount Zion and over her assemblies a cloud by day, even smoke, and the brightness of a flaming fire by night; for over all the glory will be a canopy.

Isa. 18:4 - For thus the Lord has told me, "I will look from My dwelling place quietly Like dazzling heat in the sunshine, Like a cloud of dew in the heat of harvest."

Isa. 19:1 - The oracle concerning Egypt. Behold, the Lord is riding on a swift cloud and is about to come to Egypt; The idols of Egypt will tremble at His presence, And the heart of the Egyptians will melt within them.

Isa. 25:5 - Like heat in drought, You subdue the uproar of aliens; Like heat by the shadow of a cloud, the song of the ruthless is silenced.

Isa. 44:22 - I have wiped out your transgressions like a thick cloud And your sins like a heavy mist. Return to Me, for I have redeemed you.

Isa. 60:8 - Who are these who fly like a cloud And like the doves to their lattices?

COMFORT

Isa. 12:1 - Then you will say on that day, "I will give thanks to You, O Lord; For although You were angry with me, Your anger is turned away, And You comfort me."

Isa. 22:4 - Therefore I say, "Turn your eyes away from me, Let me weep bitterly, Do not try to comfort me concerning the destruction of the daughter of my people."

Isa. 40:1 – "Comfort, O comfort My people," says your God.

Isa. 51:3 - Indeed, the Lord will comfort Zion; He will comfort all her waste places. And her wilderness He will make like Eden, And her desert like the garden of the Lord; Joy and gladness will be found in her, Thanksgiving and sound of a melody.

Isa. 51:19 - These two things have befallen you; Who will mourn for you? The devastation and destruction, famine and sword; How shall I comfort you?

Isa. 57:18 - I have seen his ways, but I will heal him; I will lead him and restore comfort to him and to his mourners.

Isa. 61:2 - To proclaim the favorable year of the Lord And the day of vengeance of our God; To comfort all who mourn.

Isa. 66:13 - As one whom his mother comforts, so I will comfort you; And you will be comforted in Jerusalem.

COMFORTED

Isa. 49:13 - Shout for joy, O heavens! And rejoice, O earth! Break forth into joyful shouting, O mountains! For the Lord has comforted His people And will have compassion on His afflicted.

Isa. 52:9 - Break forth, shout joyfully together, You waste places of Jerusalem; For the Lord has comforted His people, He has redeemed Jerusalem.

Isa. 54:11 - O afflicted one, storm-tossed, and not comforted, Behold, I will set your stones in antimony, And your foundations I will lay in sapphires.

Isa. 66:13 - As one whom his mother comforts, so I will comfort you; And you will be comforted in Jerusalem.

COMING

Isa. 13:5 - They are coming from a far country, From the farthest horizons, The Lord and His instruments of indignation, To destroy the whole land.

Isa. 13:9 - Behold, the day of the Lord is coming, Cruel, with fury and burning anger, To make the land a desolation; And He will exterminate its sinners from it.

Isa. 37:28 - But I know your sitting down And your going out and your coming in And your raging against Me.

Isa. 39:6 – "Behold, the days are coming when all that is in your house and all that your fathers have laid up in store to this day will be carried to Babylon; nothing will be left," says the Lord.

Isa. 41:22 - Let them bring forth and declare to us what is going to take place; As for the former events, declare what they were, That we may consider them and know their outcome. Or announce to us what is coming.

Isa. 44:7 - Who is like Me? Let him proclaim and declare it; Yes, let him recount it to Me in order, From the time that I established the ancient nation. And let them declare to them the things that are coming And the events that are going to take place.

Isa. 66:18 - For I know their works and their thoughts; the time is coming to gather all nations and tongues. And they shall come and see My glory.

COMPASSION

Isa. 13:18 - And their bows will mow down the young men, They will not even have compassion on the fruit of the womb, Nor will their eye pity children.

Isa. 14:1 - When the Lord will have compassion on Jacob and again choose Israel, and settle them in their own land, then strangers will join them and attach themselves to the house of Jacob.

Isa. 27:11 - When its limbs are dry, they are broken off; Women come and make a fire with them, For they are not a people of discernment, Therefore their Maker will not have compassion on them. And their Creator will not be gracious to them.

Isa. 30:18 - Therefore the Lord longs to be gracious to you, And therefore He waits on high to have compassion on you. For the Lord is a God of justice; How blessed are all those who long for Him.

Isa. 49:10 - They will not hunger or thirst, Nor will the scorching heat or sun strike them down; For He who has compassion on them will lead them And will guide them to springs of water.

Isa. 49:13 - Shout for joy, O heavens! And rejoice, O earth! Break forth into joyful shouting, O mountains! For the Lord has comforted His people And will have compassion on His afflicted.

Isa. 49:15 - Can a woman forget her nursing child And have no compassion on the son of her womb? Even these may forget, but I will not forget you.

Isa. 54:7 - For a brief moment I forsook you, But with great compassion I will gather you.

Isa. 54:8 – "In an outburst of anger I hid My face from you for a moment, But with everlasting lovingkindness I will have compassion on you," Says the Lord your Redeemer.

Isa. 54:10 – "For the mountains may be removed and the hills may shake, But My lovingkindness will not be removed from you, And My covenant of peace will not be shaken," Says the Lord who has compassion on you.

Isa. 55:7 - Let the wicked forsake his way And the unrighteous man his thoughts; And let him return to the Lord, And He will have compassion on him, And to our God, For He will abundantly pardon.

Isa. 60:10 - Foreigners will build up your walls, And their kings will minister to you; For in My wrath I struck you, And in My favor I have had compassion on you.

Isa. 63:7 - I shall make mention of the lovingkindnesses of the Lord, the praises of the Lord, According to all that the Lord has granted us, And the great goodness toward the house of Israel, Which He has granted them according to His compassion And according to the abundance of His lovingkindnesses.

Isa. 63:15 - Look down from heaven and see from Your holy and glorious habitation; Where are Your zeal and Your mighty deeds? The stirrings of Your heart and Your compassion are restrained toward me.

CONTRITE

Isa. 57:15 - For thus says the high and exalted One Who lives forever, whose name is Holy, "I dwell on a high and holy place, And also with the contrite and lowly of spirit In order to revive the spirit of the lowly And to revive the heart of the contrite."

Isa. 66:2 – "For My hand made all these things, Thus all these things came into being," declares the Lord. "But to this one I will look, To him who is humble and contrite of spirit, and who trembles at My word."

CROWN

Isa. 28:1 - Woe to the proud crown of the drunkards of Ephraim, And to the fading flower of its glorious beauty, Which is at the head of the fertile valley Of those who are overcome with wine!

Isa. 28:3 - The proud crown of the drunkards of Ephraim is trodden under foot.

Isa. 28:5 - In that day the Lord of hosts will become a beautiful crown And a glorious diadem to the remnant of His people.

Isa. 62:3 - You will also be a crown of beauty in the hand of the Lord, And a royal diadem in the hand of your God.

CRUSHED

Isa. 1:28 - But transgressors and sinners will be crushed together, And those who forsake the Lord will come to an end.

Isa. 19:10 - And the pillars of Egypt will be crushed; All the hired laborers will be grieved in soul.

Isa. 23:12 - He has said, "You shall exult no more, O crushed virgin daughter of Sidon. Arise, pass over to Cyprus; even there you will find no rest."

Isa. 28:28 - Grain for bread is crushed, Indeed, he does not continue to thresh it forever. Because the wheel of his cart and his horses eventually damage it, He does not thresh it longer.

Isa. 36:6 - Behold, you rely on the staff of this crushed reed, even on Egypt, on which if a man leans, it will go into his hand and pierce it. So is Pharaoh king of Egypt to all who rely on him.

Isa. 42:4 - He will not be disheartened or crushed Until He has established justice in the earth; And the coastlands will wait expectantly for His law.

Isa. 53:5 - But He was pierced through for our transgressions, He was crushed for our iniquities; The chastening for our well-being fell upon Him, And by His scourging we are healed.

Isa. 59:5 - They hatch adders' eggs and weave the spider's web; He who eats of their eggs dies, And from that which is crushed a snake breaks forth.

CUT

Isa. 9:10 - The bricks have fallen down, But we will rebuild with smooth stones; The sycamores have been cut down, But we will replace them with cedars.

Isa. 10:7 - Yet it does not so intend, Nor does it plan so in its heart, But rather it is its purpose to destroy And to cut off many nations.

Isa. 10:33 - Behold, the Lord, the God of hosts, will lop off the boughs with a terrible crash; Those also who are tall in stature will be cut down And those who are lofty will be abased.

Isa. 10:34 - He will cut down the thickets of the forest with an iron axe, And Lebanon will fall by the Mighty One.

Isa. 11:13 - Then the jealousy of Ephraim will depart, And those who harass Judah will be cut off; Ephraim will not be jealous of Judah, And Judah will not harass Ephraim.

Isa. 14:12 - How you have fallen from heaven, O star of the morning, son of the dawn! You have been cut down to the earth, You who have weakened the nations!

Isa. 14:22 – "I will rise up against them," declares the Lord of hosts, "and will cut off from Babylon name and survivors, offspring and posterity," declares the Lord.

Isa. 15:2 - They have gone up to the temple and to Dibon, even to the high places to weep. Moab wails over Nebo and Medeba; Everyone's head is bald and every beard is cut off.

Isa. 18:5 - For before the harvest, as soon as the bud blossoms And the flower becomes a ripening grape, Then He will cut off the sprigs with pruning knives And remove and cut away the spreading branches.

Isa. 22:25 – "In that day," declares the Lord of hosts, "the peg driven in a firm place will give way; it will even break off and fall, and the load hanging on it will be cut off, for the Lord has spoken."

Isa. 29:20 - For the ruthless will come to an end and the scorner will be finished, Indeed all who are intent on doing evil will be cut off.

Isa. 33:12 - The peoples will be burned to lime, Like cut thorns which are burned in the fire.

Isa. 37:24 - Through your servants you have reproached the Lord, And you have said, 'With my many chariots I came up to the heights of the mountains, To the remotest parts of Lebanon; And I cut down its tall cedars and its choice cypresses. And I will go to its highest peak, its thickest forest.

Isa. 45:2 - I will go before you and make the rough places smooth; I will shatter the doors of bronze and cut through their iron bars.

Isa. 48:9 - For the sake of My name I delay My wrath, And for My praise I restrain it for you, In order not to cut you off.

Isa. 48:19 - Your descendants would have been like the sand, And your offspring like its grains; Their name would never be cut off or destroyed from My presence.

Isa. 51:9 - Awake, awake, put on strength, O arm of the Lord; Awake as in the days of old, the generations of long ago. Was it not You who cut Rahab in pieces, Who pierced the dragon?

Isa. 53:8 - By oppression and judgment He was taken away; And as for His generation, who considered That He was cut off out of the land of the living For the transgression of my people, to whom the stroke was due?

Isa. 55:13 - Instead of the thorn bush the cypress will come up, And instead of the nettle the myrtle will come up, And it will be a memorial to the Lord, For an everlasting sign which will not be cut off.

Isa. 56:5 - To them I will give in My house and within My walls a memorial, And a name better than that of sons and daughters; I will give them an everlasting name which will not be cut off.

DARKNESS

Isa. 5:20 - Woe to those who call evil good, and good evil; Who substitute darkness for light and light for darkness; Who substitute bitter for sweet and sweet for bitter!

Isa. 5:30 - And it will growl over it in that day like the roaring of the sea. If one looks to the land, behold, there is darkness and distress; Even the light is darkened by its clouds.

Isa. 8:22 - Then they will look to the earth, and behold, distress and darkness, the gloom of anguish; and they will be driven away into darkness.

Isa. 9:2 - The people who walk in darkness Will see a great light; Those who live in a dark land, The light will shine on them.

Isa. 29:18 - On that day the deaf will hear words of a book, And out of their gloom and darkness the eyes of the blind will see.

Isa. 42:7 - To open blind eyes, To bring out prisoners from the dungeon And those who dwell in darkness from the prison.

Isa. 42:16 - I will lead the blind by a way they do not know, In paths they do not know I will guide them. I will make darkness into light before them And rugged places into plains. These are the things I will do, And I will not leave them undone.

Isa. 45:3 - I will give you the treasures of darkness And hidden wealth of secret places, So that you may know that it is I, The Lord, the God of Israel, who calls you by your name.

Isa. 45:7 - The One forming light and creating darkness, Causing well-being and creating calamity; I am the Lord who does all these.

Isa. 47:5 - Sit silently, and go into darkness, O daughter of the Chaldeans, For you will no longer be called The queen of kingdoms.

Isa. 49:9 - Saying to those who are bound, "Go forth," To those who are in darkness, "Show yourselves." Along the roads they will feed, And their pasture will be on all bare heights.

Isa. 50:10 - Who is among you that fears the Lord, That obeys the voice of His servant, That walks in darkness and has no light? Let him trust in the name of the Lord and rely on his God.

Isa. 58:10 - And if you give yourself to the hungry And satisfy the desire of the afflicted, Then your light will rise in darkness And your gloom will become like midday.

Isa. 59:9 - Therefore justice is far from us, And righteousness does not overtake us; We hope for light, but behold, darkness, For brightness, but we walk in gloom.

Isa. 60:2 - For behold, darkness will cover the earth And deep darkness the peoples; But the Lord will rise upon you And His glory will appear upon you.

DAY

Isa. 2:11 - The proud look of man will be abased And the loftiness of man will be humbled, And the Lord alone will be exalted in that day.

Isa. 2:12 - For the Lord of hosts will have a day of reckoning Against everyone who is proud and lofty And against everyone who is lifted up, That he may be abased.

Isa. 2:17 - The pride of man will be humbled And the loftiness of men will be abased; And the Lord alone will be exalted in that day.

Isa. 2:20 - In that day men will cast away to the moles and the bats Their idols of silver and their idols of gold, Which they made for themselves to worship…

Isa. 3:7 - He will protest on that day, saying, "I will not be your healer, For in my house there is neither bread nor cloak; You should not appoint me ruler of the people."

Isa. 3:18 - In that day the Lord will take away the beauty of their anklets, headbands, crescent ornaments.

Isa. 4:1 - For seven women will take hold of one man in that day, saying, "We will eat our own bread and wear our own clothes, only let us be called by your name; take away our reproach!"

Isa. 4:2 - In that day the Branch of the Lord will be beautiful and glorious, and the fruit of the earth will be the pride and the adornment of the survivors of Israel.

Isa. 4:5 - Then the Lord will create over the whole area of Mount Zion and over her assemblies a cloud by day, even smoke, and the brightness of a flaming fire by night; for over all the glory will be a canopy.

Isa. 4:6 - There will be a shelter to give shade from the heat by day, and refuge and protection from the storm and the rain.

Isa. 5:30 - And it will growl over it in that day like the roaring of the sea. If one looks to the land, behold, there is darkness and distress; Even the light is darkened by its clouds.

Isa. 7:17 - The Lord will bring on you, on your people, and on your father's house such days as have never come since the day that Ephraim separated from Judah, the king of Assyria.

Isa. 7:18 - In that day the Lord will whistle for the fly that is in the remotest part of the rivers of Egypt and for the bee that is in the land of Assyria.

Isa. 7:20 - In that day the Lord will shave with a razor, hired from regions beyond the Euphrates (that is, with the king of Assyria), the head and the hair of the legs; and it will also remove the beard.

Isa. 7:21 - Now in that day a man may keep alive a heifer and a pair of sheep.

Isa. 7:23 - And it will come about in that day, that every place where there used to be a thousand vines, valued at a thousand shekels of silver, will become briars and thorns.

Isa. 9:14 - So the Lord cuts off head and tail from Israel, Both palm branch and bulrush in a single day.

Isa. 10:3 - Now what will you do in the day of punishment, And in the devastation which will come from afar? To whom will you flee for help? And where will you leave your wealth?

Isa. 10:17 - And the light of Israel will become a fire and his Holy One a flame, And it will burn and devour his thorns and his briars in a single day.

Isa. 10:20 - Now in that day the remnant of Israel, and those of the house of Jacob who have escaped, will never again rely on the one who struck them, but will truly rely on the Lord, the Holy One of Israel.

Isa. 10:27 - So it will be in that day, that his burden will be removed from your shoulders and his yoke from your neck, and the yoke will be broken because of fatness.

Isa. 11:10 - Then in that day The nations will resort to the root of Jesse, Who will stand as a signal for the peoples; And His resting place will be glorious.

Isa. 11:11 - Then it will happen on that day that the Lord Will again recover the second time with His hand

The remnant of His people, who will remain, From Assyria, Egypt, Pathros, Cush, Elam, Shinar, Hamath, And from the islands of the sea.

Isa. 11:16 - And there will be a highway from Assyria For the remnant of His people who will be left, Just as there was for Israel In the day that they came up out of the land of Egypt.

Isa. 12:1 - Then you will say on that day, "I will give thanks to You, O Lord; For although You were angry with me, Your anger is turned away, And You comfort me."

Isa. 12:4 - And in that day you will say, "Give thanks to the Lord, call on His name. Make known His deeds among the peoples; Make them remember that His name is exalted."

Isa. 13:6 - Wail, for the day of the Lord is near! It will come as destruction from the Almighty.

Isa. 13:9 - Behold, the day of the Lord is coming, Cruel, with fury and burning anger, To make the land a desolation; And He will exterminate its sinners from it.

Isa. 13:13 - Therefore I will make the heavens tremble, And the earth will be shaken from its place At the fury of the Lord of hosts In the day of His burning anger.

Isa. 14:3 - And it will be in the day when the Lord gives you rest from your pain and turmoil and harsh service in which you have been enslaved.

Isa. 17:4 - Now in that day the glory of Jacob will fade, And the fatness of his flesh will become lean.

Isa. 17:7 - In that day man will have regard for his Maker And his eyes will look to the Holy One of Israel.

Isa. 17:9 - In that day their strong cities will be like forsaken places in the forest, Or like branches which they abandoned before the sons of Israel; And the land will be a desolation.

Isa. 17:11 - In the day that you plant it you carefully fence it in, And in the morning you bring your seed to blossom; But the harvest will be a heap In a day of sickliness and incurable pain.

Isa. 19:16 - In that day the Egyptians will become like women, and they will tremble and be in dread because of the waving of the hand of the Lord of hosts, which He is going to wave over them.

Isa. 19:18 - In that day five cities in the land of Egypt will be speaking the language of Canaan and swearing allegiance to the Lord of hosts; one will be called the City of Destruction.

DEAD

Isa. 8:19 - When they say to you, "Consult the mediums and the spiritists who whisper and mutter," should not a people consult their God? Should they consult the dead on behalf of the living?

Isa. 14:9 - Sheol from beneath is excited over you to meet you when you come; It arouses for you the spirits of the dead, all the leaders of the earth; It raises all the kings of the nations from their thrones.

Isa. 19:3 - Then the spirit of the Egyptians will be demoralized within them; And I will confound their strategy, So that they will resort to idols and ghosts of the dead And to mediums and spiritists.

Isa. 26:14 - The dead will not live, the departed spirits will not rise; Therefore You have punished and destroyed them, And You have wiped out all remembrance of them.

Isa. 26:19 - Your dead will live; Their corpses will rise. You who lie in the dust, awake and shout for joy, For your dew is as the dew of the dawn, And the earth will give birth to the departed spirits.

Isa. 37:36 - Then the angel of the Lord went out and struck 185,000 in the camp of the Assyrians; and when men arose early in the morning, behold, all of these were dead.

Isa. 59:10 - We grope along the wall like blind men, We grope like those who have no eyes; We stumble at midday as in the twilight, Among those who are vigorous we are like dead men.

DELIGHT

Isa. 11:3 - And He will delight in the fear of the Lord, And He will not judge by what His eyes see, Nor make a decision by what His ears hear.

Isa. 32:14 - Because the palace has been abandoned, the populated city forsaken. Hill and watch-tower have become caves forever, A delight for wild donkeys, a pasture for flocks.

Isa. 55:2 - Why do you spend money for what is not bread, And your wages for what does not satisfy? Listen carefully to Me, and eat what is good, And delight yourself in abundance.

Isa. 58:2 - Yet they seek Me day by day and delight to know My ways, As a nation that has done righteousness And has not forsaken the ordinance of their God. They ask Me for just decisions, They delight in the nearness of God.

Isa. 58:13 - If because of the sabbath, you turn your foot From doing your own pleasure on My holy day, And call the sabbath a delight, the holy day of the Lord honorable, And honor it, desisting from your own ways, From seeking your own pleasure And speaking your own word.

Isa. 58:14 - Then you will take delight in the Lord, And I will make you ride on the heights of the earth; And I will feed you with the heritage of Jacob your father, For the mouth of the Lord has spoken.

Isa. 62:4 - It will no longer be said to you, "Forsaken," Nor to your land will it any longer be said, "Desolate"; But you will be called, "My delight is in her," And your land, "Married"; For the Lord delights in you, And to Him your land will be married.

Isa. 65:12 - I will destine you for the sword, And all of you will bow down to the slaughter. Because I called, but you did not answer; I spoke, but you did not hear. And you did evil in My sight And chose that in which I did not delight.

Isa. 66:4 - So I will choose their punishments And will bring on them what they dread. Because I called, but no one answered; I spoke, but they did not listen. And they did evil in My sight And chose that in which I did not delight.

DELIVERANCE

Isa. 26:18 - We were pregnant, we writhed in labor, We gave birth, as it seems, only to wind. We could not accomplish deliverance for the earth, Nor were inhabitants of the world born.

DESTROYED

Isa. 23:1 - The oracle concerning Tyre. Wail, O ships of Tarshish, For Tyre is destroyed, without house or harbor; It is reported to them from the land of Cyprus.

Isa. 23:14 - Wail, O ships of Tarshish, For your stronghold is destroyed.

Isa. 26:14 - The dead will not live, the departed spirits will not rise; Therefore You have punished and destroyed them, And You have wiped out all remembrance of them.

Isa. 33:1 - Woe to you, O destroyer, While you were not destroyed; And he who is treacherous, while others did not deal treacherously with him. As soon as you finish destroying, you will be destroyed; As soon as you cease to deal treacherously, others will deal treacherously with you.

Isa. 34:2 - For the Lord's indignation is against all the nations, And His wrath against all their armies; He has utterly destroyed them, He has given them over to slaughter.

Isa. 37:12 - Did the gods of those nations which my fathers have destroyed deliver them, even Gozan and Haran and Rezeph and the sons of Eden who were in Telassar?

Isa. 37:19 - And have cast their gods into the fire, for they were not gods but the work of men's hands, wood and stone. So they have destroyed them.

Isa. 48:19 - Your descendants would have been like the sand, And your offspring like its grains; Their name would never be cut off or destroyed from My presence.

Isa. 49:19 - For your waste and desolate places and your destroyed land— Surely now you will be too cramped for the inhabitants, And those who swallowed you will be far away.

DESTRUCTION

Isa. 10:22 - For though your people, O Israel, may be like the sand of the sea, Only a remnant within them will return; A destruction is determined, overflowing with righteousness.

Isa. 10:23 - For a complete destruction, one that is decreed, the Lord God of hosts will execute in the midst of the whole land.

Isa. 10:25 - For in a very little while My indignation against you will be spent and My anger will be directed to their destruction.

Isa. 13:6 - Wail, for the day of the Lord is near! It will come as destruction from the Almighty.

Isa. 14:23 – "I will also make it a possession for the hedgehog and swamps of water, and I will sweep it with the broom of destruction," declares the Lord of hosts.

Isa. 16:4 - Let the outcasts of Moab stay with you; Be a hiding place to them from the destroyer. For the extortioner has come to an end, destruction has ceased, Oppressors have completely disappeared from the land.

Isa. 19:18 - In that day five cities in the land of Egypt will be speaking the language of Canaan and swearing allegiance to the Lord of hosts; one will be called the City of Destruction.

Isa. 22:4 - Therefore I say, "Turn your eyes away from me, Let me weep bitterly, Do not try to comfort me concerning the destruction of the daughter of my people."

Isa. 28:2 - Behold, the Lord has a strong and mighty agent; As a storm of hail, a tempest of destruction, Like a storm of mighty overflowing waters, He has cast it down to the earth with His hand.

Isa. 28:22 - And now do not carry on as scoffers, Or your fetters will be made stronger; For I have heard from the Lord God of hosts Of decisive destruction on all the earth.

Isa. 34:5 - For My sword is satiated in heaven, Behold it shall descend for judgment upon Edom And upon the people whom I have devoted to destruction.

Isa. 47:11 - But evil will come on you Which you will not know how to charm away; And disaster will fall on you For which you cannot atone; And destruction about which you do not know Will come on you suddenly.

Isa. 51:19 - These two things have befallen you; Who will mourn for you? The devastation and destruction, famine and sword; How shall I comfort you?

Isa. 59:7 - Their feet run to evil, And they hasten to shed innocent blood; Their thoughts are thoughts of iniquity, Devastation and destruction are in their highways.

Isa. 60:18 - Violence will not be heard again in your land, Nor devastation or destruction within your borders; But you will call your walls salvation, and your gates praise.

DISEASE
Isa. 10:16 - Therefore the Lord, the God of hosts, will send a wasting disease among his stout warriors; And under his glory a fire will be kindled like a burning flame.

DISMAYED
Isa. 20:5 - Then they will be dismayed and ashamed because of Cush their hope and Egypt their boast.

Isa. 37:27 - Therefore their inhabitants were short of strength, They were dismayed and put to shame; They were as the vegetation of the field and as the green herb, As grass on the housetops is scorched before it is grown up.

Isa. 51:7 - Listen to Me, you who know righteousness, A people in whose heart is My law; Do not fear the reproach of man, Nor be dismayed at their revilings.

DOGS

Isa. 56:10 - His watchmen are blind, All of them know nothing. All of them are mute dogs unable to bark, Dreamers lying down, who love to slumber.

Isa. 56:11 - And the dogs are greedy, they are not satisfied. And they are shepherds who have no understanding; They have all turned to their own way, Each one to his unjust gain, to the last one.

DRAW

Isa. 5:19 - Who say, "Let Him make speed, let Him hasten His work, that we may see it; And let the purpose of the Holy One of Israel draw near And come to pass, that we may know it!"

Isa. 12:3 - Therefore you will joyously draw water From the springs of salvation.

Isa. 29:13 - Then the Lord said, "Because this people draw near with their words And honor Me with their lip service, But they remove their hearts far from Me, And their reverence for Me consists of tradition learned by rote."

Isa. 34:1 - Draw near, O nations, to hear; and listen, O peoples! Let the earth and all it contains hear, and the world and all that springs from it.

Isa. 44:25 - Causing the omens of boasters to fail, Making fools out of diviners, Causing wise men to draw back And turning their knowledge into foolishness.

Isa. 45:20 - Gather yourselves and come; Draw near together, you fugitives of the nations; They have no knowledge, Who carry about their wooden idol And pray to a god who cannot save.

Isa. 50:8 - He who vindicates Me is near; Who will contend with Me? Let us stand up to each other; Who has a case against Me? Let him draw near to Me.

DREAD

Isa. 7:16 - For before the boy will know enough to refuse evil and choose good, the land whose two kings you dread will be forsaken.

Isa. 8:12 - You are not to say, "It is a conspiracy!" In regard to all that this people call a conspiracy, And you are not to fear what they fear or be in dread of it.

Isa. 8:13 - It is the Lord of hosts whom you should regard as holy. And He shall be your fear, And He shall be your dread.

Isa. 19:16 - In that day the Egyptians will become like women, and they will tremble and be in dread because of the waving of the hand of the Lord of hosts, which He is going to wave over them.

Isa. 19:17 - The land of Judah will become a terror to Egypt; everyone to whom it is mentioned will be in dread of it, because of the purpose of the Lord of hosts which He is purposing against them.

Isa. 66:4 - So I will choose their punishments And will bring on them what they dread. Because I called, but no one answered; I spoke, but they did not listen. And they did evil in My sight And chose that in which I did not delight.

DRUNKARDS

Isa. 28:1 - Woe to the proud crown of the drunkards of Ephraim, And to the fading flower of its glorious beauty, Which is at the head of the fertile valley Of those who are overcome with wine!

Isa. 28:3 - The proud crown of the drunkards of Ephraim is trodden under foot.

DUST

Isa. 2:10 - Enter the rock and hide in the dust From the terror of the Lord and from the splendor of His majesty.

Isa. 5:24 - Therefore, as a tongue of fire consumes stubble And dry grass collapses into the flame, So their root will become like rot and their blossom blow away as dust; For they have rejected the law of the Lord of hosts And despised the word of the Holy One of Israel.

Isa. 17:13 - The nations rumble on like the rumbling of many waters, But He will rebuke them and they will flee far away, And be chased like chaff in the mountains before the wind, Or like whirling dust before a gale.

Isa. 25:12 - The unassailable fortifications of your walls He will bring down, Lay low and cast to the ground, even to the dust.

Isa. 26:5 - For He has brought low those who dwell on high, the unassailable city; He lays it low, He lays it low to the ground, He casts it to the dust.

Isa. 26:19 - Your dead will live; Their corpses will rise. You who lie in the dust, awake and shout for joy, For your dew is as the dew of the dawn, And the earth will give birth to the departed spirits.

Isa. 29:4 - Then you will be brought low; From the earth you will speak, And from the dust where you are prostrate Your words will come. Your voice will also be like that of a spirit from the ground, And your speech will whisper from the dust.

Isa. 29:5 - But the multitude of your enemies will become like fine dust, And the multitude of the ruthless ones like the chaff which blows away; And it will happen instantly, suddenly.

Isa. 34:7 - Wild oxen will also fall with them And young bulls with strong ones; Thus their land will be soaked with blood, And their dust become greasy with fat.

Isa. 40:12 - Who has measured the waters in the hollow of His hand, And marked off the heavens by the span, And calculated the dust of the earth by the measure, And weighed the mountains in a balance And the hills in a pair of scales?

Isa. 40:15 - Behold, the nations are like a drop from a bucket, And are regarded as a speck of dust on the scales; Behold, He lifts up the islands like fine dust.

Isa. 41:2 - Who has aroused one from the east Whom He calls in righteousness to His feet? He delivers up nations before him And subdues kings. He makes them like dust with his sword, As the wind-driven chaff with his bow.

Isa. 47:1 - Come down and sit in the dust, O virgin daughter of Babylon; Sit on the ground without a throne, O daughter of the Chaldeans! For you shall no longer be called tender and delicate.

Isa. 49:23 - Kings will be your guardians, And their princesses your nurses. They will bow down to you with their faces to the earth And lick the dust of your feet; And you will know that I am the Lord; Those who hopefully wait for Me will not be put to shame.

Isa. 52:2 - Shake yourself from the dust, rise up, O captive Jerusalem; Loose yourself from the chains around your neck, O captive daughter of Zion.

Isa. 65:25 – "The wolf and the lamb will graze together, and the lion will eat straw like the ox; and dust will be the serpent's food. They will do no evil or harm in all My holy mountain," says the Lord.

EARS

Isa. 5:9 - In my ears the Lord of hosts has sworn, "Surely, many houses shall become desolate, Even great and fine ones, without occupants."

Isa. 6:10 - Render the hearts of this people insensitive, Their ears dull, And their eyes dim, Otherwise they might see with their eyes, Hear with their ears, Understand with their hearts, And return and be healed.

Isa. 11:3 - And He will delight in the fear of the Lord, And He will not judge by what His eyes see, Nor make a decision by what His ears hear.

Isa. 17:5 - It will be even like the reaper gathering the standing grain, As his arm harvests the ears, Or it will be like one gleaning ears of grain In the valley of Rephaim.

Isa. 30:21 - Your ears will hear a word behind you, "This is the way, walk in it," whenever you turn to the right or to the left.

Isa. 32:3 - Then the eyes of those who see will not be blinded, And the ears of those who hear will listen.

Isa. 33:15 - He who walks righteously and speaks with sincerity, He who rejects unjust gain And shakes his hands so that they hold no bribe; He who stops his ears from hearing about bloodshed And shuts his eyes from looking upon evil.

Isa. 35:5 - Then the eyes of the blind will be opened And the ears of the deaf will be unstopped.

Isa. 37:29 - Because of your raging against Me And because your arrogance has come up to My ears, Therefore I will put My hook in your nose And My bridle in your lips, And I will turn you back by the way which you came.

Isa. 42:20 - You have seen many things, but you do not observe them; Your ears are open, but none hears.

Isa. 43:8 - Bring out the people who are blind, even though they have eyes, And the deaf, even though they have ears.
Isa. 49:20 - The children of whom you were bereaved will yet say in your ears, "The place is too cramped for me; Make room for me that I may live here."

ENDURE
Isa. 1:13 - Bring your worthless offerings no longer, Incense is an abomination to Me. New moon and sabbath, the calling of assemblies— I cannot endure iniquity and the solemn assembly.
Isa. 66:22 – "For just as the new heavens and the new earth Which I make will endure before Me," declares the Lord, "So your offspring and your name will endure."

ENLARGE
Isa. 54:2 - Enlarge the place of your tent; Stretch out the curtains of your dwellings, spare not; Lengthen your cords And strengthen your pegs.

ESTEEMED
Isa. 2:22 - Stop regarding man, whose breath of life is in his nostrils; For why should he be esteemed?
Isa. 53:4 - Surely our griefs He Himself bore, And our sorrows He carried; Yet we ourselves esteemed Him stricken, Smitten of God, and afflicted.

EVERLASTING
Isa. 24:5 - The earth is also polluted by its inhabitants, for they transgressed laws, violated statutes, broke the everlasting covenant.
Isa. 26:4 - Trust in the Lord forever, For in God the Lord, we have an everlasting Rock.

Isa. 35:10 - And the ransomed of the Lord will return And come with joyful shouting to Zion, With everlasting joy upon their heads. They will find gladness and joy, And sorrow and sighing will flee away.

Isa. 40:28 - Do you not know? Have you not heard? The Everlasting God, the Lord, the Creator of the ends of the earth Does not become weary or tired. His understanding is inscrutable.

Isa. 45:17 - Israel has been saved by the Lord With an everlasting salvation; You will not be put to shame or humiliated To all eternity.

Isa. 51:11 - So the ransomed of the Lord will return And come with joyful shouting to Zion, And everlasting joy will be on their heads. They will obtain gladness and joy, And sorrow and sighing will flee away.

Isa. 54:8 – "In an outburst of anger I hid My face from you for a moment, But with everlasting lovingkindness I will have compassion on you," Says the Lord your Redeemer.

Isa. 55:3 - Incline your ear and come to Me. Listen, that you may live; And I will make an everlasting covenant with you, According to the faithful mercies shown to David.

Isa. 55:13 - Instead of the thorn bush the cypress will come up, And instead of the nettle the myrtle will come up, And it will be a memorial to the Lord, For an everlasting sign which will not be cut off.

Isa. 56:5 - To them I will give in My house and within My walls a memorial, And a name better than that of sons and daughters; I will give them an everlasting name which will not be cut off.

Isa. 60:15 - Whereas you have been forsaken and hated With no one passing through, I will make you an

everlasting pride, A joy from generation to generation.
Isa. 60:19 - No longer will you have the sun for light by day, Nor for brightness will the moon give you light; But you will have the Lord for an everlasting light, And your God for your glory.

Isa. 60:20 - Your sun will no longer set, Nor will your moon wane; For you will have the Lord for an everlasting light, And the days of your mourning will be over.

Isa. 61:7 - Instead of your shame you will have a double portion, And instead of humiliation they will shout for joy over their portion. Therefore they will possess a double portion in their land, Everlasting joy will be theirs.

Isa. 61:8 - For I, the Lord, love justice, I hate robbery in the burnt offering; And I will faithfully give them their recompense And make an everlasting covenant with them.

Isa. 63:12 - Who caused His glorious arm to go at the right hand of Moses, Who divided the waters before them to make for Himself an everlasting name.

EXULT

Isa. 23:12 - He has said, "You shall exult no more, O crushed virgin daughter of Sidon. Arise, pass over to Cyprus; even there you will find no rest."

Isa. 61:10 - I will rejoice greatly in the Lord, My soul will exult in my God; For He has clothed me with garments of salvation, He has wrapped me with a robe of righteousness, As a bridegroom decks himself with a garland, And as a bride adorns herself with her jewels.

EYES

Isa. 1:15 - So when you spread out your hands in prayer, I will hide My eyes from you; Yes, even though you multiply prayers, I will not listen. Your hands are covered with blood.

Isa. 3:16 - Moreover, the Lord said, "Because the daughters of Zion are proud And walk with heads held high and seductive eyes, And go along with mincing steps And tinkle the bangles on their feet."

Isa. 5:15 - So the common man will be humbled and the man of importance abased, The eyes of the proud also will be abased.

Isa. 5:21 - Woe to those who are wise in their own eyes And clever in their own sight!

Isa. 6:5 - Then I said, "Woe is me, for I am ruined! Because I am a man of unclean lips, And I live among a people of unclean lips; For my eyes have seen the King, the Lord of hosts."

Isa. 6:10 - Render the hearts of this people insensitive, Their ears dull, And their eyes dim, Otherwise they might see with their eyes, Hear with their ears, Understand with their hearts, And return and be healed.

Isa. 11:3 - And He will delight in the fear of the Lord, And He will not judge by what His eyes see, Nor make a decision by what His ears hear.

Isa. 13:16 - Their little ones also will be dashed to pieces Before their eyes; Their houses will be plundered And their wives ravished.

Isa. 17:7 - In that day man will have regard for his Maker And his eyes will look to the Holy One of Israel.

Isa. 22:4 - Therefore I say, "Turn your eyes away from me, Let me weep bitterly, Do not try to comfort me concerning the destruction of the daughter of my people."

Isa. 29:10 - For the Lord has poured over you a spirit of deep sleep, He has shut your eyes, the prophets; And He has covered your heads, the seers.

Isa. 29:18 - On that day the deaf will hear words of a book, And out of their gloom and darkness the eyes of the blind will see.

Isa. 30:20 - Although the Lord has given you bread of privation and water of oppression, He, your Teacher will no longer hide Himself, but your eyes will behold your Teacher.

Isa. 32:3 - Then the eyes of those who see will not be blinded, And the ears of those who hear will listen.

Isa. 33:15 - He who walks righteously and speaks with sincerity, He who rejects unjust gain And shakes his hands so that they hold no bribe; He who stops his ears from hearing about bloodshed And shuts his eyes from looking upon evil.

Isa. 33:17 - Your eyes will see the King in His beauty; They will behold a far-distant land.

Isa. 33:20 - Look upon Zion, the city of our appointed feasts; Your eyes will see Jerusalem, an undisturbed habitation, A tent which will not be folded; Its stakes will never be pulled up, Nor any of its cords be torn apart.

Isa. 35:5 - Then the eyes of the blind will be opened And the ears of the deaf will be unstopped.

Isa. 37:17 - Incline Your ear, O Lord, and hear; open Your eyes, O Lord, and see; and listen to all the words of Sennacherib, who sent them to reproach the living God.

Isa. 37:23 - Whom have you reproached and blasphemed? And against whom have you raised your voice And haughtily lifted up your eyes? Against the Holy One of Israel!

Isa. 38:14 - Like a swallow, like a crane, so I twitter; I moan like a dove; My eyes look wistfully to the heights; O Lord, I am oppressed, be my security.

Isa. 40:26 - Lift up your eyes on high And see who has created these stars, The One who leads forth their host by number, He calls them all by name; Because of the greatness of His might and the strength of His power, Not one of them is missing.

Isa. 42:7 - To open blind eyes, To bring out prisoners from the dungeon And those who dwell in darkness from the prison.

Isa. 43:8 - Bring out the people who are blind, even though they have eyes, And the deaf, even though they have ears.

Isa. 44:18 - They do not know, nor do they understand, for He has smeared over their eyes so that they cannot see and their hearts so that they cannot comprehend.

Isa. 49:18 – "Lift up your eyes and look around; All of them gather together, they come to you. As I live," declares the Lord, "You will surely put on all of them as jewels and bind them on as a bride."

Isa. 51:6 - Lift up your eyes to the sky, Then look to the earth beneath; For the sky will vanish like smoke, And the earth will wear out like a garment And its inhabitants will die in like manner; But My salvation will be forever, And My righteousness will not wane.

Isa. 52:8 - Listen! Your watchmen lift up their voices, They shout joyfully together; For they will see with their own eyes When the Lord restores Zion.

Isa. 59:10 - We grope along the wall like blind men, We grope like those who have no eyes; We stumble at midday as in the twilight, Among those who are vigorous we are like dead men.

Isa. 60:4 - Lift up your eyes round about and see; They all gather together, they come to you. Your sons will come from afar, And your daughters will be carried in the arms.

FADING

Isa. 28:1 - Woe to the proud crown of the drunkards of Ephraim, And to the fading flower of its glorious beauty, Which is at the head of the fertile valley Of those who are overcome with wine!

Isa. 28:4 - And the fading flower of its glorious beauty, Which is at the head of the fertile valley, Will be like the first-ripe fig prior to summer, Which one sees, And as soon as it is in his hand, He swallows it.

FALLEN

Isa. 3:8 - For Jerusalem has stumbled and Judah has fallen, Because their speech and their actions are against the Lord, To rebel against His glorious presence.

Isa. 9:10 - The bricks have fallen down, But we will rebuild with smooth stones; The sycamores have been cut down, But we will replace them with cedars.

Isa. 14:12 - How you have fallen from heaven, O star of the morning, son of the dawn! You have been cut down to the earth, You who have weakened the nations!

Isa. 16:9 - Therefore I will weep bitterly for Jazer, for the vine of Sibmah; I will drench you with my tears, O Heshbon and Elealeh; For the shouting over your summer fruits and your harvest has fallen away.

Isa. 17:1 - The oracle concerning Damascus. "Behold, Damascus is about to be removed from being a city And will become a fallen ruin.

Isa. 21:9 - Now behold, here comes a troop of riders, horsemen in pairs. And one said, "Fallen, fallen is Babylon; And all the images of her gods are shattered on the ground."

FAST

Isa. 47:12 - Stand fast now in your spells And in your many sorceries With which you have labored from your youth; Perhaps you will be able to profit, Perhaps you may cause trembling.

Isa. 56:4 - For thus says the Lord, "To the eunuchs who keep My sabbaths, And choose what pleases Me, And hold fast My covenant."

Isa. 56:6 - Also the foreigners who join themselves to the Lord, To minister to Him, and to love the name of the Lord, To be His servants, every one who keeps from profaning the sabbath And holds fast My covenant.

Isa. 58:3 - Why have we fasted and You do not see? Why have we humbled ourselves and You do not notice?' Behold, on the day of your fast you find your desire, And drive hard all your workers.

Isa. 58:4 - Behold, you fast for contention and strife and to strike with a wicked fist. You do not fast like you do today to make your voice heard on high.

Isa. 58:5 - Is it a fast like this which I choose, a day for a man to humble himself? Is it for bowing one's head like a reed And for spreading out sackcloth and ashes as a bed? Will you call this a fast, even an acceptable day to the Lord?

Isa. 58:6 - Is this not the fast which I choose, To loosen the bonds of wickedness, To undo the bands of the yoke, And to let the oppressed go free And break every yoke?

FAVOR

Isa. 26:10 - Though the wicked is shown favor, He does not learn righteousness; He deals unjustly in the land of uprightness, And does not perceive the majesty of the Lord.

Isa. 60:10 - Foreigners will build up your walls, And their kings will minister to you; For in My wrath I struck you, And in My favor I have had compassion on you.

FIRST

Isa. 1:26 - Then I will restore your judges as at the first, And your counselors as at the beginning; After that you will be called the city of righteousness, A faithful city.

Isa. 28:4 - And the fading flower of its glorious beauty, Which is at the head of the fertile valley, Will be like the first-ripe fig prior to summer, Which one sees, And as soon as it is in his hand, He swallows it.

Isa. 41:4 - Who has performed and accomplished it, Calling forth the generations from the beginning? "I, the Lord, am the first, and with the last. I am He."

Isa. 43:27 - Your first forefather sinned, And your spokesmen have transgressed against Me.

Isa. 44:6 - Thus says the Lord, the King of Israel and his Redeemer, the Lord of hosts: "I am the first and I am the last, And there is no God besides Me."

Isa. 48:12 - Listen to Me, O Jacob, even Israel whom I called; I am He, I am the first, I am also the last.

Isa. 48:16 - Come near to Me, listen to this: From the first I have not spoken in secret, From the time it took place, I was there. And now the Lord God has sent Me, and His Spirit.

Isa. 52:4 - For thus says the Lord God, "My people went down at the first into Egypt to reside there; then the Assyrian oppressed them without cause."

Isa. 60:9 - Surely the coastlands will wait for Me; And the ships of Tarshish will come first, To bring your sons from afar, Their silver and their gold with them,

For the name of the Lord your God, And for the Holy One of Israel because He has glorified you.

FLINT
Isa. 5:28 - Its arrows are sharp and all its bows are bent; The hoofs of its horses seem like flint and its chariot wheels like a whirlwind.
Isa. 50:7 - For the Lord God helps Me, Therefore, I am not disgraced; Therefore, I have set My face like flint, And I know that I will not be ashamed.

FOOD
Isa. 23:18 - Her gain and her harlot's wages will be set apart to the Lord; it will not be stored up or hoarded, but her gain will become sufficient food and choice attire for those who dwell in the presence of the Lord.
Isa. 62:8 - The Lord has sworn by His right hand and by His strong arm, "I will never again give your grain as food for your enemies; Nor will foreigners drink your new wine for which you have labored."
Isa. 65:25 – "The wolf and the lamb will graze together, and the lion will eat straw like the ox; and dust will be the serpent's food. They will do no evil or harm in all My holy mountain," says the Lord.

FOOTSTOOL
Isa. 66:1 - Thus says the Lord, "Heaven is My throne and the earth is My footstool. Where then is a house you could build for Me? And where is a place that I may rest?"

FRUITFUL
Isa. 10:18 - And He will destroy the glory of his forest and of his fruitful garden, both soul and body, And it will be as when a sick man wastes away.

Isa. 16:10 - Gladness and joy are taken away from the fruitful field; In the vineyards also there will be no cries of joy or jubilant shouting, No treader treads out wine in the presses, For I have made the shouting to cease.

Isa. 17:6 - Yet gleanings will be left in it like the shaking of an olive tree, Two or three olives on the topmost bough, Four or five on the branches of a fruitful tree, Declares the Lord, the God of Israel.

Isa. 32:12 - Beat your breasts for the pleasant fields, for the fruitful vine.

GARDEN

Isa. 1:30 - For you will be like an oak whose leaf fades away Or as a garden that has no water.

Isa. 10:18 - And He will destroy the glory of his forest and of his fruitful garden, both soul and body, And it will be as when a sick man wastes away.

Isa. 51:3 - Indeed, the Lord will comfort Zion; He will comfort all her waste places. And her wilderness He will make like Eden, And her desert like the garden of the Lord; Joy and gladness will be found in her, Thanksgiving and sound of a melody.

Isa. 58:11 - And the Lord will continually guide you, And satisfy your desire in scorched places, And give strength to your bones; And you will be like a watered garden, And like a spring of water whose waters do not fail.

Isa. 61:11 - For as the earth brings forth its sprouts, And as a garden causes the things sown in it to spring up, So the Lord God will cause righteousness and praise To spring up before all the nations.

GLORY

Isa. 4:5 - Then the Lord will create over the whole area of Mount Zion and over her assemblies a cloud by day, even smoke, and the brightness of a flaming fire by night; for over all the glory will be a canopy.

Isa. 6:3 - And one called out to another and said, "Holy, Holy, Holy, is the Lord of hosts, The whole earth is full of His glory."

Isa. 8:7 - Now therefore, behold, the Lord is about to bring on them the strong and abundant waters of the Euphrates, Even the king of Assyria and all his glory; And it will rise up over all its channels and go over all its banks.

Isa. 10:16 - Therefore the Lord, the God of hosts, will send a wasting disease among his stout warriors; And under his glory a fire will be kindled like a burning flame.

Isa. 10:18 - And He will destroy the glory of his forest and of his fruitful garden, both soul and body, And it will be as when a sick man wastes away.

Isa. 13:19 - And Babylon, the beauty of kingdoms, the glory of the Chaldeans' pride, Will be as when God overthrew Sodom and Gomorrah.

Isa. 14:18 - All the kings of the nations lie in glory, Each in his own tomb.

Isa. 16:14 - But now the Lord speaks, saying, "Within three years, as a hired man would count them, the glory of Moab will be degraded along with all his great population, and his remnant will be very small and impotent."

Isa. 17:3 – "The fortified city will disappear from Ephraim, And sovereignty from Damascus And the remnant of Aram; They will be like the glory of the sons of Israel," Declares the Lord of hosts.

Isa. 17:4 - Now in that day the glory of Jacob will fade, And the fatness of his flesh will become lean.

Isa. 22:23 - I will drive him like a peg in a firm place, And he will become a throne of glory to his father's house.

Isa. 22:24 - So they will hang on him all the glory of his father's house, offspring and issue, all the least of vessels, from bowls to all the jars.

Isa. 24:16 - From the ends of the earth we hear songs, "Glory to the Righteous One," But I say, "Woe to me! Woe to me! Alas for me! The treacherous deal treacherously, And the treacherous deal very treacherously."

Isa. 24:23 - Then the moon will be abashed and the sun ashamed, For the Lord of hosts will reign on Mount Zion and in Jerusalem, And His glory will be before His elders.

Isa. 35:2 - It will blossom profusely And rejoice with rejoicing and shout of joy. The glory of Lebanon will be given to it, The majesty of Carmel and Sharon. They will see the glory of the Lord, The majesty of our God.

Isa. 40:5 - Then the glory of the Lord will be revealed, And all flesh will see it together; For the mouth of the Lord has spoken.

Isa. 41:16 You will winnow them, and the wind will carry them away, And the storm will scatter them; But you will rejoice in the Lord, You will glory in the Holy One of Israel.

Isa. 42:8 - I am the Lord, that is My name; I will not give My glory to another, Nor My praise to graven images.

Isa. 42:12 Let them give glory to the Lord And declare His praise in the coastlands.

Isa. 43:7 - Everyone who is called by My name, And whom I have created for My glory, Whom I have formed, even whom I have made.

Isa. 44:23 - Shout for joy, O heavens, for the Lord has done it! Shout joyfully, you lower parts of the earth; Break forth into a shout of joy, you mountains, O forest, and every tree in it; For the Lord has redeemed Jacob And in Israel He shows forth His glory.

Isa. 45:25 - In the Lord all the offspring of Israel Will be justified and will glory.

Isa. 46:13 - I bring near My righteousness, it is not far off; And My salvation will not delay. And I will grant salvation in Zion, And My glory for Israel.

Isa. 48:11 - For My own sake, for My own sake, I will act; For how can My name be profaned? And My glory I will not give to another.

Isa. 49:3 - He said to Me, "You are My Servant, Israel, In Whom I will show My glory."

Isa. 58:8 - Then your light will break out like the dawn, And your recovery will speedily spring forth; And your righteousness will go before you; The glory of the Lord will be your rear guard.

Isa. 59:19 - So they will fear the name of the Lord from the west And His glory from the rising of the sun, For He will come like a rushing stream Which the wind of the Lord drives.

Isa. 60:1 - Arise, shine; for your light has come, And the glory of the Lord has risen upon you.

Isa. 60:2 - For behold, darkness will cover the earth And deep darkness the peoples; But the Lord will rise upon you And His glory will appear upon you.

Isa. 60:13 - The glory of Lebanon will come to you, The juniper, the box tree and the cypress together, To beautify the place of My sanctuary; And I shall make the place of My feet glorious.

Isa. 60:19 - No longer will you have the sun for light by day, Nor for brightness will the moon give you light; But you will have the Lord for an everlasting light, And your God for your glory.

Isa. 62:2 - The nations will see your righteousness, And all kings your glory; And you will be called by a new name Which the mouth of the Lord will designate.

Isa. 66:12 - For thus says the Lord, "Behold, I extend peace to her like a river, And the glory of the nations like an overflowing stream; And you will be nursed, you will be carried on the hip and fondled on the knees."

Isa. 66:18 - For I know their works and their thoughts; the time is coming to gather all nations and tongues. And they shall come and see My glory.

Isa. 66:19 - I will set a sign among them and will send survivors from them to the nations: Tarshish, Put, Lud, Meshech, Rosh, Tubal and Javan, to the distant coastlands that have neither heard My fame nor seen My glory. And they will declare My glory among the nations.

GRACIOUS

Isa. 27:11 - When its limbs are dry, they are broken off; Women come and make a fire with them, For they are not a people of discernment, Therefore their Maker will not have compassion on them. And their Creator will not be gracious to them.

Isa. 30:18 - Therefore the Lord longs to be gracious to you, And therefore He waits on high to have compassion on you. For the Lord is a God of justice; How blessed are all those who long for Him.

Isa. 30:19 - O people in Zion, inhabitant in Jerusalem, you will weep no longer. He will surely be gracious to you at the sound of your cry; when He hears it, He will answer you.

Isa. 33:2 - O Lord, be gracious to us; we have waited for You. Be their strength every morning, Our salvation also in the time of distress.

GREEDY
Isa. 56:11 - And the dogs are greedy, they are not satisfied. And they are shepherds who have no understanding; They have all turned to their own way, Each one to his unjust gain, to the last one.

GUARD
Isa. 21:8 - Then the lookout called, "O Lord, I stand continually by day on the watchtower, And I am stationed every night at my guard post."

Isa. 27:3 - I, the Lord, am its keeper; I water it every moment. So that no one will damage it, I guard it night and day.

Isa. 52:12 - But you will not go out in haste, Nor will you go as fugitives; For the Lord will go before you, And the God of Israel will be your rear guard.

Isa. 58:8 - Then your light will break out like the dawn, And your recovery will speedily spring forth; And your righteousness will go before you; The glory of the Lord will be your rear guard.

GUIDE
Isa. 3:12 - O My people! Their oppressors are children, And women rule over them. O My people! Those who guide you lead you astray And confuse the direction of your paths.

Isa. 9:16 - For those who guide this people are leading them astray; And those who are guided by them are brought to confusion.

Isa. 42:16 - I will lead the blind by a way they do not know, In paths they do not know I will guide them. I will make darkness into light before them And rugged places into plains. These are the things I will do, And I will not leave them undone.

Isa. 49:10 - They will not hunger or thirst, Nor will the scorching heat or sun strike them down; For He who has compassion on them will lead them And will guide them to springs of water.

Isa. 51:18 - There is none to guide her among all the sons she has borne, Nor is there one to take her by the hand among all the sons she has reared.

Isa. 58:11 - And the Lord will continually guide you, And satisfy your desire in scorched places, And give strength to your bones; And you will be like a watered garden, And like a spring of water whose waters do not fail.

HAUGHTINESS

Isa. 10:12 - So it will be that when the Lord has completed all His work on Mount Zion and on Jerusalem, He will say, "I will punish the fruit of the arrogant heart of the king of Assyria and the pomp of his haughtiness."

Isa. 13:11 - Thus I will punish the world for its evil And the wicked for their iniquity; I will also put an end to the arrogance of the proud And abase the haughtiness of the ruthless.

HEAL

Isa. 19:22 - The Lord will strike Egypt, striking but healing; so they will return to the Lord, and He will respond to them and will heal them.

Isa. 57:18 - I have seen his ways, but I will heal him; I will lead him and restore comfort to him and to his mourners.

Isa. 57:19 – "Creating the praise of the lips. Peace, peace to him who is far and to him who is near," Says the Lord, "and I will heal him."

HEAVENS

Isa. 1:2 - Listen, O heavens, and hear, O earth; For the Lord speaks, "Sons I have reared and brought up, But they have revolted against Me."

Isa. 13:13 - Therefore I will make the heavens tremble, And the earth will be shaken from its place At the fury of the Lord of hosts In the day of His burning anger.

Isa. 40:12 - Who has measured the waters in the hollow of His hand, And marked off the heavens by the span, And calculated the dust of the earth by the measure, And weighed the mountains in a balance And the hills in a pair of scales?

Isa. 40:22 - It is He who sits above the circle of the earth, And its inhabitants are like grasshoppers, Who stretches out the heavens like a curtain And spreads them out like a tent to dwell in.

Isa. 42:5 - Thus says God the Lord, Who created the heavens and stretched them out, Who spread out the earth and its offspring, Who gives breath to the people on it And spirit to those who walk in it.

Isa. 44:23 - Shout for joy, O heavens, for the Lord has done it! Shout joyfully, you lower parts of the earth; Break forth into a shout of joy, you mountains, O forest, and every tree in it; For the Lord has redeemed Jacob And in Israel He shows forth His glory.

Isa. 44:24 - Thus says the Lord, your Redeemer, and the one who formed you from the womb, "I, the Lord, am the maker of all things, Stretching out the heavens by Myself And spreading out the earth all alone."

Isa. 45:8 - Drip down, O heavens, from above, And let the clouds pour down righteousness; Let the earth open up and salvation bear fruit, And righteousness spring up with it. I, the Lord, have created it.

Isa. 45:12 - It is I who made the earth, and created man upon it. I stretched out the heavens with My hands And I ordained all their host.

Isa. 45:18 - For thus says the Lord, who created the heavens (He is the God who formed the earth and made it, He established it and did not create it a waste place, but formed it to be inhabited), "I am the Lord, and there is none else."

Isa. 48:13 - Surely My hand founded the earth, And My right hand spread out the heavens; When I call to them, they stand together.

Isa. 49:13 Shout for joy, O heavens! And rejoice, O earth! Break forth into joyful shouting, O mountains! For the Lord has comforted His people And will have compassion on His afflicted.

Isa. 50:3 - I clothe the heavens with blackness And make sackcloth their covering.

Isa. 51:13 - That you have forgotten the Lord your Maker, Who stretched out the heavens And laid the foundations of the earth, That you fear continually all day long because of the fury of the oppressor, As he makes ready to destroy? But where is the fury of the oppressor?

Isa. 51:16 - I have put My words in your mouth and have covered you with the shadow of My hand, to establish the heavens, to found the earth, and to say to Zion, "You are My people."

Isa. 55:9 - For as the heavens are higher than the earth, So are My ways higher than your ways And My thoughts than your thoughts.

Isa. 64:1 - Oh, that You would rend the heavens and come down, That the mountains might quake at Your presence.

Isa. 65:17 - For behold, I create new heavens and a new earth; And the former things will not be remembered or come to mind.

Isa. 66:22 – "For just as the new heavens and the new earth Which I make will endure before Me," declares the Lord, "So your offspring and your name will endure."

HOLY

Isa. 1:4 - Alas, sinful nation, People weighed down with iniquity, Offspring of evildoers, Sons who act corruptly! They have abandoned the Lord, They have despised the Holy One of Israel, They have turned away from Him.

Isa. 4:3 - It will come about that he who is left in Zion and remains in Jerusalem will be called holy — everyone who is recorded for life in Jerusalem.

Isa. 5:16 - But the Lord of hosts will be exalted in judgment, And the holy God will show Himself holy in righteousness.

Isa. 5:19 - Who say, "Let Him make speed, let Him hasten His work, that we may see it; And let the purpose of the Holy One of Israel draw near And come to pass, that we may know it!"

Isa. 5:24 - Therefore, as a tongue of fire consumes stubble And dry grass collapses into the flame, So their root will become like rot and their blossom blow away as dust; For they have rejected the law of the Lord of hosts And despised the word of the Holy One of Israel.

Isa. 6:3 - And one called out to another and said, "Holy, Holy, Holy, is the Lord of hosts, The whole earth is full of His glory."

Isa. 6:13 - Yet there will be a tenth portion in it, And it will again be subject to burning, Like a terebinth or an oak Whose stump remains when it is felled. The holy seed is its stump.

Isa. 8:13 - It is the Lord of hosts whom you should regard as holy. And He shall be your fear, And He shall be your dread.

Isa. 10:17 - And the light of Israel will become a fire and his Holy One a flame, And it will burn and devour his thorns and his briars in a single day.

Isa. 10:20 - Now in that day the remnant of Israel, and those of the house of Jacob who have escaped, will never again rely on the one who struck them, but will truly rely on the Lord, the Holy One of Israel.

Isa. 11:9 - They will not hurt or destroy in all My holy mountain, For the earth will be full of the knowledge of the Lord As the waters cover the sea.

Isa. 12:6 - Cry aloud and shout for joy, O inhabitant of Zion, For great in your midst is the Holy One of Israel.

Isa. 17:7 - In that day man will have regard for his Maker And his eyes will look to the Holy One of Israel.

Isa. 27:13 - It will come about also in that day that a great trumpet will be blown, and those who were perishing in the land of Assyria and who were scattered in the land of Egypt will come and worship the Lord in the holy mountain at Jerusalem.

Isa. 29:19 - The afflicted also will increase their gladness in the Lord, And the needy of mankind will rejoice in the Holy One of Israel.

Isa. 29:23 - But when he sees his children, the work of My hands, in his midst, They will sanctify My name;

Indeed, they will sanctify the Holy One of Jacob And will stand in awe of the God of Israel.

Isa. 30:11 - Get out of the way, turn aside from the path, Let us hear no more about the Holy One of Israel.

Isa. 30:12 - Therefore thus says the Holy One of Israel, "Since you have rejected this word And have put your trust in oppression and guile, and have relied on them."

Isa. 30:15 - For thus the Lord God, the Holy One of Israel, has said, "In repentance and rest you will be saved, In quietness and trust is your strength." But you were not willing.

Isa. 31:1 - Woe to those who go down to Egypt for help And rely on horses, And trust in chariots because they are many And in horsemen because they are very strong, But they do not look to the Holy One of Israel, nor seek the Lord!

Isa. 37:23 - Whom have you reproached and blasphemed? And against whom have you raised your voice And haughtily lifted up your eyes? Against the Holy One of Israel!

Isa. 40:25 – "To whom then will you liken Me That I would be his equal?" says the Holy One.

Isa. 41:14 – "Do not fear, you worm Jacob, you men of Israel; I will help you," declares the Lord, "and your Redeemer is the Holy One of Israel."

Isa. 41:16 - You will winnow them, and the wind will carry them away, And the storm will scatter them; But you will rejoice in the Lord, You will glory in the Holy One of Israel.

Isa. 41:20 - That they may see and recognize, And consider and gain insight as well, That the hand of the Lord has done this, And the Holy One of Israel has created it.

Isa. 43:3 - For I am the Lord your God, The Holy One of Israel, your Savior; I have given Egypt as your ransom, Cush and Seba in your place.

Isa. 43:14 - Thus says the Lord your Redeemer, the Holy One of Israel, "For your sake I have sent to Babylon, And will bring them all down as fugitives, Even the Chaldeans, into the ships in which they rejoice."

Isa. 43:15 - I am the Lord, your Holy One, The Creator of Israel, your King.

Isa. 45:11 - Thus says the Lord, the Holy One of Israel, and his Maker: "Ask Me about the things to come concerning My sons, And you shall commit to Me the work of My hands."

Isa. 47:4 - Our Redeemer, the Lord of hosts is His name, The Holy One of Israel.

Isa. 48:2 - For they call themselves after the holy city And lean on the God of Israel; The Lord of hosts is His name.

Isa. 48:17 - Thus says the Lord, your Redeemer, the Holy One of Israel, "I am the Lord your God, who teaches you to profit, Who leads you in the way you should go."

Isa. 49:7 - Thus says the Lord, the Redeemer of Israel and its Holy One, To the despised One, To the One abhorred by the nation, To the Servant of rulers, "Kings will see and arise, Princes will also bow down, Because of the Lord who is faithful, the Holy One of Israel who has chosen You."

Isa. 52:1 - Awake, awake, Clothe yourself in your strength, O Zion; Clothe yourself in your beautiful garments, O Jerusalem, the holy city; For the uncircumcised and the unclean Will no longer come into you.

Isa. 52:10 - The Lord has bared His holy arm In the sight of all the nations, That all the ends of the earth may see The salvation of our God.

Isa. 54:5 - For your husband is your Maker, Whose name is the Lord of hosts; And your Redeemer is the Holy One of Israel, Who is called the God of all the earth.

Isa. 55:5 - Behold, you will call a nation you do not know, And a nation which knows you not will run to you, Because of the Lord your God, even the Holy One of Israel; For He has glorified you.

Isa. 56:7 - Even those I will bring to My holy mountain And make them joyful in My house of prayer. Their burnt offerings and their sacrifices will be acceptable on My altar; For My house will be called a house of prayer for all the peoples.

Isa. 57:13 - When you cry out, let your collection of idols deliver you. But the wind will carry all of them up, And a breath will take them away. But he who takes refuge in Me will inherit the land And will possess My holy mountain.

Isa. 57:15 - For thus says the high and exalted One Who lives forever, whose name is Holy, "I dwell on a high and holy place, And also with the contrite and lowly of spirit In order to revive the spirit of the lowly And to revive the heart of the contrite."

Isa. 58:13 - If because of the sabbath, you turn your foot From doing your own pleasure on My holy day, And call the sabbath a delight, the holy day of the Lord honorable, And honor it, desisting from your own ways, From seeking your own pleasure And speaking your own word.

Isa. 60:9 - Surely the coastlands will wait for Me; And the ships of Tarshish will come first, To bring your sons from afar, Their silver and their gold with them,

For the name of the Lord your God, And for the Holy One of Israel because He has glorified you.

Isa. 60:14 - The sons of those who afflicted you will come bowing to you, And all those who despised you will bow themselves at the soles of your feet; And they will call you the city of the Lord, The Zion of the Holy One of Israel.

HOPELESS

Isa. 57:10 - You were tired out by the length of your road, Yet you did not say, 'It is hopeless.' You found renewed strength, Therefore you did not faint.

HOW

Isa. 1:21 - How the faithful city has become a harlot, She who was full of justice! Righteousness once lodged in her, But now murderers.

Isa. 6:11 - Then I said, "Lord, how long?" And He answered, "Until cities are devastated and without inhabitant, Houses are without people And the land is utterly desolate."

Isa. 8:4 - For before the boy knows how to cry out "My father" or "My mother," the wealth of Damascus and the spoil of Samaria will be carried away before the king of Assyria.

Isa. 14:4 - That you will take up this taunt against the king of Babylon, and say, "How the oppressor has ceased, And how fury has ceased!"

Isa. 14:12 - How you have fallen from heaven, O star of the morning, son of the dawn! You have been cut down to the earth, You who have weakened the nations!

Isa. 14:32 - How then will one answer the messengers of the nation? That the Lord has founded Zion, And the afflicted of His people will seek refuge in it.

Isa. 19:11 - The princes of Zoan are mere fools; The advice of Pharaoh's wisest advisers has become stupid. How can you men say to Pharaoh, "I am a son of the wise, a son of ancient kings"?

Isa. 20:6 - So the inhabitants of this coastland will say in that day, 'Behold, such is our hope, where we fled for help to be delivered from the king of Assyria; and we, how shall we escape?'

Isa. 21:11 - The oracle concerning Edom. One keeps calling to me from Seir, "Watchman, how far gone is the night? Watchman, how far gone is the night?"

Isa. 30:18 - Therefore the Lord longs to be gracious to you, And therefore He waits on high to have compassion on you. For the Lord is a God of justice; How blessed are all those who long for Him.

Isa. 32:20 - How blessed will you be, you who sow beside all waters, Who let out freely the ox and the donkey.

Isa. 36:9 - How then can you repulse one official of the least of my master's servants and rely on Egypt for chariots and for horsemen?

Isa. 38:3 - And said, "Remember now, O Lord, I beseech You, how I have walked before You in truth and with a whole heart, and have done what is good in Your sight." And Hezekiah wept bitterly.

Isa. 47:11 - But evil will come on you Which you will not know how to charm away; And disaster will fall on you For which you cannot atone; And destruction about which you do not know Will come on you suddenly.

Isa. 48:11 - For My own sake, for My own sake, I will act; For how can My name be profaned? And My glory I will not give to another.

Isa. 50:4 - The Lord God has given Me the tongue of disciples, That I may know how to sustain the weary one with a word. He awakens Me morning by morning, He awakens My ear to listen as a disciple.

Isa. 51:19 - These two things have befallen you; Who will mourn for you? The devastation and destruction, famine and sword; How shall I comfort you?

Isa. 52:7 - How lovely on the mountains Are the feet of him who brings good news, Who announces peace And brings good news of happiness, Who announces salvation, And says to Zion, "Your God reigns!"

Isa. 56:2 - How blessed is the man who does this, And the son of man who takes hold of it; Who keeps from profaning the sabbath, And keeps his hand from doing any evil.

IDOLS

Isa. 2:8 - Their land has also been filled with idols; They worship the work of their hands, That which their fingers have made.

Isa. 2:18 - But the idols will completely vanish.

Isa. 2:20 - In that day men will cast away to the moles and the bats Their idols of silver and their idols of gold, Which they made for themselves to worship…

Isa. 10:10 - As my hand has reached to the kingdoms of the idols, Whose graven images were greater than those of Jerusalem and Samaria.

Isa. 10:11 - Shall I not do to Jerusalem and her images Just as I have done to Samaria and her idols?

Isa. 19:1 - The oracle concerning Egypt. Behold, the Lord is riding on a swift cloud and is about to come to Egypt; The idols of Egypt will tremble at His presence, And the heart of the Egyptians will melt within them.

Isa. 19:3 - Then the spirit of the Egyptians will be demoralized within them; And I will confound their strategy, So that they will resort to idols and ghosts of the dead And to mediums and spiritists.

Isa. 31:7 - For in that day every man will cast away his silver idols and his gold idols, which your sinful hands have made for you as a sin.

Isa. 42:17 - They will be turned back and be utterly put to shame, Who trust in idols, Who say to molten images, "You are our gods."

Isa. 45:16 - They will be put to shame and even humiliated, all of them; The manufacturers of idols will go away together in humiliation.

Isa. 57:13 - When you cry out, let your collection of idols deliver you. But the wind will carry all of them up, And a breath will take them away. But he who takes refuge in Me will inherit the land And will possess My holy mountain.

IMMANUEL

Isa. 7:14 - Therefore the Lord Himself will give you a sign: Behold, a virgin will be with child and bear a son, and she will call His name Immanuel.

Isa. 8:8 - Then it will sweep on into Judah, it will overflow and pass through, It will reach even to the neck; And the spread of its wings will fill the breadth of your land, O Immanuel.

INIQUITIES

Isa. 43:24 - You have bought Me not sweet cane with money, Nor have you filled Me with the fat of your sacrifices; Rather you have burdened Me with your sins, You have wearied Me with your iniquities.

Isa. 50:1 - Thus says the Lord, "Where is the certificate of divorce By which I have sent your mother away? Or to whom of My creditors did I sell you? Behold, you were sold for your iniquities, And for your transgressions your mother was sent away."

Isa. 53:5 - But He was pierced through for our transgressions, He was crushed for our iniquities; The chastening for our well-being fell upon Him, And by His scourging we are healed.

Isa. 53:11 - As a result of the anguish of His soul, He will see it and be satisfied; By His knowledge the Righteous One, My Servant, will justify the many, As He will bear their iniquities.

Isa. 59:2 - But your iniquities have made a separation between you and your God, And your sins have hidden His face from you so that He does not hear.

Isa. 59:12 - For our transgressions are multiplied before You, And our sins testify against us; For our transgressions are with us, And we know our iniquities.

Isa. 64:6 - For all of us have become like one who is unclean, And all our righteous deeds are like a filthy garment; And all of us wither like a leaf, And our iniquities, like the wind, take us away.

Isa. 64:7 - There is no one who calls on Your name, Who arouses himself to take hold of You; For You have hidden Your face from us And have delivered us into the power of our iniquities.

Isa. 65:7 – "Both their own iniquities and the iniquities of their fathers together," says the Lord. "Because they have burned incense on the mountains And scorned Me on the hills, Therefore I will measure their former work into their bosom."

JESSE

Isa. 11:1 - Then a shoot will spring from the stem of Jesse, And a branch from his roots will bear fruit.

Isa. 11:10 - Then in that day The nations will resort to the root of Jesse, Who will stand as a signal for the peoples; And His resting place will be glorious.

JOY

Isa. 12:6 - Cry aloud and shout for joy, O inhabitant of Zion, For great in your midst is the Holy One of Israel.

Isa. 14:7 - The whole earth is at rest and is quiet; They break forth into shouts of joy.

Isa. 16:10 Gladness and joy are taken away from the fruitful field; In the vineyards also there will be no cries of joy or jubilant shouting, No treader treads out wine in the presses, For I have made the shouting to cease.

Isa. 24:11 - There is an outcry in the streets concerning the wine; All joy turns to gloom. The gaiety of the earth is banished.

Isa. 24:14 - They raise their voices, they shout for joy; They cry out from the west concerning the majesty of the Lord.

Isa. 26:19 - Your dead will live; Their corpses will rise. You who lie in the dust, awake and shout for joy, For your dew is as the dew of the dawn, And the earth will give birth to the departed spirits.

Isa. 35:2 - It will blossom profusely And rejoice with rejoicing and shout of joy. The glory of Lebanon will be given to it, The majesty of Carmel and Sharon. They will see the glory of the Lord, The majesty of our God.

Isa. 35:6 - Then the lame will leap like a deer, And the tongue of the mute will shout for joy. For waters will break forth in the wilderness And streams in the Arabah.

Isa. 35:10 - And the ransomed of the Lord will return And come with joyful shouting to Zion, With everlasting joy upon their heads. They will find gladness and joy, And sorrow and sighing will flee away.

Isa. 42:11 - Let the wilderness and its cities lift up their voices, The settlements where Kedar inhabits. Let the inhabitants of Sela sing aloud, Let them shout for joy from the tops of the mountains.

Isa. 44:23 - Shout for joy, O heavens, for the Lord has done it! Shout joyfully, you lower parts of the earth; Break forth into a shout of joy, you mountains, O forest, and every tree in it; For the Lord has redeemed Jacob And in Israel He shows forth His glory.

Isa. 49:13 - Shout for joy, O heavens! And rejoice, O earth! Break forth into joyful shouting, O mountains! For the Lord has comforted His people And will have compassion on His afflicted.

Isa. 51:3 - Indeed, the Lord will comfort Zion; He will comfort all her waste places. And her wilderness He will make like Eden, And her desert like the garden of the Lord; Joy and gladness will be found in her, Thanksgiving and sound of a melody.

Isa. 51:11 - So the ransomed of the Lord will return And come with joyful shouting to Zion, And everlasting joy will be on their heads. They will obtain gladness and joy, And sorrow and sighing will flee away.

Isa. 54:1 – "Shout for joy, O barren one, you who have borne no child; Break forth into joyful shouting and cry aloud, you who have not travailed; For the sons of the desolate one will be more numerous Than the sons of the married woman," says the Lord.

Isa. 55:12 - For you will go out with joy And be led forth with peace; The mountains and the hills will break forth into shouts of joy before you, And all the trees of the field will clap their hands.

Isa. 60:15 - Whereas you have been forsaken and hated With no one passing through, I will make you an everlasting pride, A joy from generation to generation.

Isa. 61:7 - Instead of your shame you will have a double portion, And instead of humiliation they will shout for joy over their portion. Therefore they will possess a double portion in their land, Everlasting joy will be theirs.

Isa. 66:5 - Hear the word of the Lord, you who tremble at His word: Your brothers who hate you, who exclude you for My name's sake, Have said, "Let the Lord be glorified, that we may see your joy.' But they will be put to shame."

JOYFUL

Isa. 32:13 - For the land of my people in which thorns and briars shall come up; Yea, for all the joyful houses and for the jubilant city.

Isa. 35:10 - And the ransomed of the Lord will return And come with joyful shouting to Zion, With everlasting joy upon their heads. They will find gladness and joy, And sorrow and sighing will flee away.

Isa. 48:20 - Go forth from Babylon! Flee from the Chaldeans! Declare with the sound of joyful shouting, proclaim this, Send it out to the end of the earth; Say, "The Lord has redeemed His servant Jacob."

Isa. 49:13 - Shout for joy, O heavens! And rejoice, O earth! Break forth into joyful shouting, O mountains! For the Lord has comforted His people And will have compassion on His afflicted.

Isa. 51:11 - So the ransomed of the Lord will return And come with joyful shouting to Zion, And everlasting joy will be on their heads. They will obtain gladness and joy, And sorrow and sighing will flee away.

Isa. 54:1 – "Shout for joy, O barren one, you who have borne no child; Break forth into joyful shouting and cry aloud, you who have not travailed; For the sons of the desolate one will be more numerous Than the sons of the married woman," says the Lord.

Isa. 56:7 - Even those I will bring to My holy mountain And make them joyful in My house of prayer. Their burnt offerings and their sacrifices will be acceptable on My altar; For My house will be called a house of prayer for all the peoples.

Isa. 66:10 - Be joyful with Jerusalem and rejoice for her, all you who love her; Be exceedingly glad with her, all you who mourn over her.

JUDGMENT

Isa. 3:14 - The Lord enters into judgment with the elders and princes of His people, "It is you who have devoured the vineyard; The plunder of the poor is in your houses."

Isa. 4:4 - When the Lord has washed away the filth of the daughters of Zion and purged the bloodshed of Jerusalem from her midst, by the spirit of judgment and the spirit of burning.

Isa. 5:16 - But the Lord of hosts will be exalted in judgment, And the holy God will show Himself holy in righteousness.

Isa. 28:6 - A spirit of justice for him who sits in judgment, A strength to those who repel the onslaught at the gate.

Isa. 28:7 - And these also reel with wine and stagger from strong drink: The priest and the prophet reel with strong drink, They are confused by wine, they stagger from strong drink; They reel while having visions, They totter when rendering judgment.

Isa. 34:5 - For My sword is satiated in heaven, Behold it shall descend for judgment upon Edom And upon the people whom I have devoted to destruction.

Isa. 41:1 - Coastlands, listen to Me in silence, And let the peoples gain new strength; Let them come forward, then let them speak; Let us come together for judgment.

Isa. 53:8 - By oppression and judgment He was taken away; And as for His generation, who considered That He was cut off out of the land of the living For the transgression of my people, to whom the stroke was due?

Isa. 54:17 – "No weapon that is formed against you will prosper; And every tongue that accuses you in judgment you will condemn. This is the heritage of the servants of the Lord, And their vindication is from Me," declares the Lord.

Isa. 66:16 - For the Lord will execute judgment by fire And by His sword on all flesh, And those slain by the Lord will be many.

LAID

Isa. 14:8 - Even the cypress trees rejoice over you, and the cedars of Lebanon, saying, "Since you were laid low, no tree cutter comes up against us."

Isa. 24:3 - The earth will be completely laid waste and completely despoiled, for the Lord has spoken this word.

Isa. 32:19 - And it will hail when the forest comes down, And the city will be utterly laid low.

Isa. 39:6 – "Behold, the days are coming when all that is in your house and all that your fathers have laid up in store to this day will be carried to Babylon; nothing will be left," says the Lord.

Isa. 44:28 - It is I who says of Cyrus, "He is My shepherd! And he will perform all My desire." And he declares of Jerusalem, "She will be built," And of the temple, "Your foundation will be laid."

Isa. 51:13 - That you have forgotten the Lord your Maker, Who stretched out the heavens And laid the foundations of the earth, That you fear continually all day long because of the fury of the oppressor, As he makes ready to destroy? But where is the fury of the oppressor?

LAMB

Isa. 11:6 - And the wolf will dwell with the lamb, And the leopard will lie down with the young goat, And the calf and the young lion and the fatling together; And a little boy will lead them.

Isa. 16:1 - Send the tribute lamb to the ruler of the land, From Sela by way of the wilderness to the mountain of the daughter of Zion.

Isa. 53:7 - He was oppressed and He was afflicted, Yet He did not open His mouth; Like a lamb that is led to slaughter, And like a sheep that is silent before its shearers, So He did not open His mouth.

Isa. 65:25 – "The wolf and the lamb will graze together, and the lion will eat straw like the ox; and dust will be the serpent's food. They will do no evil or harm in all My holy mountain," says the Lord.

Isa. 66:3 - But he who kills an ox is like one who slays a man; He who sacrifices a lamb is like the one who breaks a dog's neck; He who offers a grain offering is like one who offers swine's blood; He who burns incense is like the one who blesses an idol. As they have chosen their own ways, And their soul delights in their abominations.

LAST

Isa. 2:2 - Now it will come about that In the last days The mountain of the house of the Lord Will be established as the chief of the mountains, And will be raised above the hills; And all the nations will stream to it.

Isa. 7:9 - And the head of Ephraim is Samaria and the head of Samaria is the son of Remaliah. If you will not believe, you surely shall not last.

Isa. 41:4 – Who has performed and accomplished it, Calling forth the generations from the beginning? "I, the Lord, am the first, and with the last. I am He."

Isa. 44:6 - Thus says the Lord, the King of Israel and his Redeemer, the Lord of hosts: 'I am the first and I am the last, And there is no God besides Me.

Isa. 48:12 - Listen to Me, O Jacob, even Israel whom I called; I am He, I am the first, I am also the last.

Isa. 56:11 - And the dogs are greedy, they are not satisfied. And they are shepherds who have no understanding; They have all turned to their own way, Each one to his unjust gain, to the last one.

LEAD

Isa. 3:12 - O My people! Their oppressors are children, And women rule over them. O My people! Those who guide you lead you astray And confuse the direction of your paths.

Isa. 11:6 - And the wolf will dwell with the lamb, And the leopard will lie down with the young goat, And the calf and the young lion and the fatling together; And a little boy will lead them.

Isa. 20:4 - So the king of Assyria will lead away the captives of Egypt and the exiles of Cush, young and old, naked and barefoot with buttocks uncovered, to the shame of Egypt.

Isa. 40:11 - Like a shepherd He will tend His flock, In His arm He will gather the lambs And carry them in His bosom; He will gently lead the nursing ewes.

Isa. 42:16 - I will lead the blind by a way they do not know, In paths they do not know I will guide them. I will make darkness into light before them And rugged places into plains. These are the things I will do, And I will not leave them undone.

Isa. 49:10 - They will not hunger or thirst, Nor will the scorching heat or sun strike them down; For He who has compassion on them will lead them And will guide them to springs of water.

Isa. 57:18 - I have seen his ways, but I will heal him; I will lead him and restore comfort to him and to his mourners.

LIGHT

Isa. 2:5 - Come, house of Jacob, and let us walk in the light of the Lord.

Isa. 5:20 - Woe to those who call evil good, and good evil; Who substitute darkness for light and light for darkness; Who substitute bitter for sweet and sweet for bitter!

Isa. 5:30 - And it will growl over it in that day like the roaring of the sea. If one looks to the land, behold, there is darkness and distress; Even the light is darkened by its clouds.

Isa. 9:2 - The people who walk in darkness Will see a great light; Those who live in a dark land, The light will shine on them.

Isa. 10:17 - And the light of Israel will become a fire and his Holy One a flame, And it will burn and devour his thorns and his briars in a single day.

Isa. 13:10 - For the stars of heaven and their constellations Will not flash forth their light; The sun will be dark when it rises And the moon will not shed its light.

Isa. 30:26 - The light of the moon will be as the light of the sun, and the light of the sun will be seven times brighter, like the light of seven days, on the day the Lord binds up the fracture of His people and heals the bruise He has inflicted.

Isa. 42:6 - I am the Lord, I have called you in righteousness, I will also hold you by the hand and watch over you, And I will appoint you as a covenant to the people, As a light to the nations.

Isa. 42:16 - I will lead the blind by a way they do not know, In paths they do not know I will guide them. I will make darkness into light before them And rugged places into plains. These are the things I will do, And I will not leave them undone.

Isa. 45:7 - The One forming light and creating darkness, Causing well-being and creating calamity; I am the Lord who does all these.

Isa. 49:6 - He says, "It is too small a thing that You should be My Servant To raise up the tribes of Jacob and to restore the preserved ones of Israel; I will also make You a light of the nations So that My salvation may reach to the end of the earth."

Isa. 50:10 - Who is among you that fears the Lord, That obeys the voice of His servant, That walks in darkness and has no light? Let him trust in the name of the Lord and rely on his God.

Isa. 50:11 - Behold, all you who kindle a fire, Who encircle yourselves with firebrands, Walk in the light of your fire And among the brands you have set ablaze. This you will have from My hand: You will lie down in torment.

Isa. 51:4 - Pay attention to Me, O My people, And give ear to Me, O My nation; For a law will go forth from Me, And I will set My justice for a light of the peoples.

Isa. 58:8 - Then your light will break out like the dawn, And your recovery will speedily spring forth; And your righteousness will go before you; The glory of the Lord will be your rear guard.

Isa. 58:10 - And if you give yourself to the hungry And satisfy the desire of the afflicted, Then your light will rise in darkness And your gloom will become like midday.

Isa. 59:9 - Therefore justice is far from us, And righteousness does not overtake us; We hope for light, but behold, darkness, For brightness, but we walk in gloom.

Isa. 60:1 - Arise, shine; for your light has come, And the glory of the Lord has risen upon you.

Isa. 60:3 - Nations will come to your light, And kings to the brightness of your rising.

Isa. 60:19 - No longer will you have the sun for light by day, Nor for brightness will the moon give you light; But you will have the Lord for an everlasting light, And your God for your glory.

Isa. 60:20 - Your sun will no longer set, Nor will your moon wane; For you will have the Lord for an everlasting light, And the days of your mourning will be over.

LIVE

Isa. 5:8 - Woe to those who add house to house and join field to field, Until there is no more room, So that you have to live alone in the midst of the land!

Isa. 6:5 - Then I said, "Woe is me, for I am ruined! Because I am a man of unclean lips, And I live among a people of unclean lips; For my eyes have seen the King, the Lord of hosts."

Isa. 9:2 - The people who walk in darkness Will see a great light; Those who live in a dark land, The light will shine on them.

Isa. 13:21 - But desert creatures will lie down there, And their houses will be full of owls; Ostriches also will live there, and shaggy goats will frolic there.

Isa. 24:6 - Therefore, a curse devours the earth, and those who live in it are held guilty. Therefore, the inhabitants of the earth are burned, and few men are left.

Isa. 26:14 - The dead will not live, the departed spirits will not rise; Therefore You have punished and destroyed them, And You have wiped out all remembrance of them.

Isa. 26:19 - Your dead will live; Their corpses will rise. You who lie in the dust, awake and shout for joy, For your dew is as the dew of the dawn, And the earth will give birth to the departed spirits.

Isa. 32:18 - Then my people will live in a peaceful habitation, And in secure dwellings and in undisturbed resting places.

Isa. 33:14 - Sinners in Zion are terrified; Trembling has seized the godless. Who among us can live with the consuming fire? Who among us can live with continual burning?

Isa. 38:1 - In those days Hezekiah became mortally ill. And Isaiah the prophet the son of Amoz came to him and said to him, "Thus says the Lord, 'Set your house in order, for you shall die and not live.'"

Isa. 38:16 - O Lord, by these things men live, And in all these is the life of my spirit; O restore me to health and let me live!

Isa. 49:18 – "Lift up your eyes and look around; All of them gather together, they come to you. As I live," declares the Lord, "You will surely put on all of them as jewels and bind them on as a bride."

Isa. 49:20 - The children of whom you were bereaved will yet say in your ears, "The place is too cramped for me; Make room for me that I may live here."

Isa. 55:3 - Incline your ear and come to Me. Listen, that you may live; And I will make an everlasting covenant with you, According to the faithful mercies shown to David.

Isa. 65:20 - No longer will there be in it an infant who lives but a few days, Or an old man who does not live out his days; For the youth will die at the age of one hundred And the one who does not reach the age of one hundred Will be thought accursed.

LIVING

Isa. 8:19 - When they say to you, "Consult the mediums and the spiritists who whisper and mutter," should not a people consult their God? Should they consult the dead on behalf of the living?

Isa. 37:4 - Perhaps the Lord your God will hear the words of Rabshakeh, whom his master the king of Assyria has sent to reproach the living God, and will rebuke the words which the Lord your God has heard. Therefore, offer a prayer for the remnant that is left.

Isa. 37:17 - Incline Your ear, O Lord, and hear; open Your eyes, O Lord, and see; and listen to all the words of Sennacherib, who sent them to reproach the living God.

Isa. 38:11 - I said, "I will not see the Lord, The Lord in the land of the living; I will look on man no more among the inhabitants of the world."

Isa. 38:19 - It is the living who give thanks to You, as I do today; A father tells his sons about Your faithfulness.

Isa. 53:8 - By oppression and judgment He was taken away; And as for His generation, who considered That He was cut off out of the land of the living For the transgression of my people, to whom the stroke was due?

LOOSEN
Isa. 20:2 - At that time the Lord spoke through Isaiah the son of Amoz, saying, "Go and loosen the sackcloth from your hips and take your shoes off your feet." And he did so, going naked and barefoot.
Isa. 58:6 - Is this not the fast which I choose, To loosen the bonds of wickedness, To undo the bands of the yoke, And to let the oppressed go free And break every yoke?

MERCIES
Isa. 55:3 - Incline your ear and come to Me. Listen, that you may live; And I will make an everlasting covenant with you, According to the faithful mercies shown to David.

MILK
Isa. 7:22 - And because of the abundance of the milk produced he will eat curds, for everyone that is left within the land will eat curds and honey.
Isa. 28:9 - To whom would He teach knowledge, And to whom would He interpret the message? Those just weaned from milk? Those just taken from the breast?
Isa. 55:1 - Ho! Every one who thirsts, come to the waters; And you who have no money come, buy and eat. Come, buy wine and milk Without money and without cost.
Isa. 60:16 - You will also suck the milk of nations And suck the breast of kings; Then you will know that I, the

Lord, am your Savior And your Redeemer, the Mighty One of Jacob.

MONEY
Isa. 3:22 - Festal robes, outer tunics, cloaks, money purses.
Isa. 43:24 - You have bought Me not sweet cane with money, Nor have you filled Me with the fat of your sacrifices; Rather you have burdened Me with your sins, You have wearied Me with your iniquities.
Isa. 52:3 - For thus says the Lord, "You were sold for nothing and you will be redeemed without money."
Isa. 55:1 - Ho! Every one who thirsts, come to the waters; And you who have no money come, buy and eat. Come, buy wine and milk Without money and without cost.
Isa. 55:2 - Why do you spend money for what is not bread, And your wages for what does not satisfy? Listen carefully to Me, and eat what is good, And delight yourself in abundance.

NATION
Isa. 1:4 - Alas, sinful nation, People weighed down with iniquity, Offspring of evildoers, Sons who act corruptly! They have abandoned the Lord, They have despised the Holy One of Israel, They have turned away from Him.
Isa. 2:4 - And He will judge between the nations, And will render decisions for many peoples; And they will hammer their swords into plowshares and their spears into pruning hooks. Nation will not lift up sword against nation, And never again will they learn war.
Isa. 5:26 - He will also lift up a standard to the distant nation, And will whistle for it from the ends of the earth; And behold, it will come with speed swiftly.

Isa. 9:3 - You shall multiply the nation, You shall increase their gladness; They will be glad in Your presence As with the gladness of harvest, As men rejoice when they divide the spoil.

Isa. 10:6 - I send it against a godless nation And commission it against the people of My fury To capture booty and to seize plunder, And to trample them down like mud in the streets.

Isa. 14:32 - How then will one answer the messengers of the nation? That the Lord has founded Zion, And the afflicted of His people will seek refuge in it.

Isa. 18:2 - Which sends envoys by the sea, Even in papyrus vessels on the surface of the waters. Go, swift messengers, to a nation tall and smooth, To a people feared far and wide, A powerful and oppressive nation Whose land the rivers divide.

Isa. 18:7 - At that time a gift of homage will be brought to the Lord of hosts From a people tall and smooth, Even from a people feared far and wide, A powerful and oppressive nation, Whose land the rivers divide — To the place of the name of the Lord of hosts, even Mount Zion.

Isa. 26:2 - Open the gates, that the righteous nation may enter, The one that remains faithful.

Isa. 26:15 - You have increased the nation, O Lord, You have increased the nation, You are glorified; You have extended all the borders of the land.

Isa. 44:7 - Who is like Me? Let him proclaim and declare it; Yes, let him recount it to Me in order, From the time that I established the ancient nation. And let them declare to them the things that are coming And the events that are going to take place.

Isa. 49:7 - Thus says the Lord, the Redeemer of Israel and its Holy One, To the despised One, To the One abhorred by the nation, To the Servant of rulers,

"Kings will see and arise, Princes will also bow down, Because of the Lord who is faithful, the Holy One of Israel who has chosen You."

Isa. 51:4 - Pay attention to Me, O My people, And give ear to Me, O My nation; For a law will go forth from Me, And I will set My justice for a light of the peoples.

Isa. 55:5 - Behold, you will call a nation you do not know, And a nation which knows you not will run to you, Because of the Lord your God, even the Holy One of Israel; For He has glorified you.

Isa. 58:2 - Yet they seek Me day by day and delight to know My ways, As a nation that has done righteousness And has not forsaken the ordinance of their God. They ask Me for just decisions, They delight in the nearness of God.

Isa. 60:12 - For the nation and the kingdom which will not serve you will perish, And the nations will be utterly ruined.

Isa. 60:22 - The smallest one will become a clan, And the least one a mighty nation. I, the Lord, will hasten it in its time.

Isa. 65:1 - I permitted Myself to be sought by those who did not ask for Me; I permitted Myself to be found by those who did not seek Me. I said, "Here am I, here am I," To a nation which did not call on My name.

Isa. 66:8 - Who has heard such a thing? Who has seen such things? Can a land be born in one day? Can a nation be brought forth all at once? As soon as Zion travailed, she also brought forth her sons.

NEAR

Isa. 5:19 - Who say, "Let Him make speed, let Him hasten His work, that we may see it; And let the purpose of the Holy One of Israel draw near And come to pass, that we may know it!"

Isa. 13:6 - Wail, for the day of the Lord is near! It will come as destruction from the Almighty.

Isa. 19:19 - In that day there will be an altar to the Lord in the midst of the land of Egypt, and a pillar to the Lord near its border.

Isa. 29:13 - Then the Lord said, "Because this people draw near with their words And honor Me with their lip service, But they remove their hearts far from Me, And their reverence for Me consists of tradition learned by rote."

Isa. 33:13 - You who are far away, hear what I have done; And you who are near, acknowledge My might.

Isa. 34:1 - Draw near, O nations, to hear; and listen, O peoples! Let the earth and all it contains hear, and the world and all that springs from it.

Isa. 41:5 - The coastlands have seen and are afraid; The ends of the earth tremble; They have drawn near and have come.

Isa. 45:20 - Gather yourselves and come; Draw near together, you fugitives of the nations; They have no knowledge, Who carry about their wooden idol And pray to a god who cannot save.

Isa. 46:13 - I bring near My righteousness, it is not far off; And My salvation will not delay. And I will grant salvation in Zion, And My glory for Israel.

Isa. 48:16 - Come near to Me, listen to this: From the first I have not spoken in secret, From the time it took place, I was there. And now the Lord God has sent Me, and His Spirit.

Isa. 50:8 - He who vindicates Me is near; Who will contend with Me? Let us stand up to each other; Who has a case against Me? Let him draw near to Me.

Isa. 51:5 - My righteousness is near, My salvation has gone forth, And My arms will judge the peoples; The coastlands will wait for Me, And for My arm they will wait expectantly.

Isa. 54:14 - In righteousness you will be established; You will be far from oppression, for you will not fear; And from terror, for it will not come near you.

Isa. 55:6 - Seek the Lord while He may be found; Call upon Him while He is near.

Isa. 57:19 – "Creating the praise of the lips. Peace, peace to him who is far and to him who is near," Says the Lord, "and I will heal him."

Isa. 65:5 - Who say, "Keep to yourself, do not come near me, For I am holier than you!" These are smoke in My nostrils, A fire that burns all the day.

NEW

Isa. 1:13 - Bring your worthless offerings no longer, Incense is an abomination to Me. New moon and sabbath, the calling of assemblies— I cannot endure iniquity and the solemn assembly.

Isa. 1:14 - I hate your new moon festivals and your appointed feasts, They have become a burden to Me; I am weary of bearing them.

Isa. 24:7 - The new wine mourns, The vine decays, All the merry-hearted sigh.

Isa. 36:17 - Until I come and take you away to a land like your own land, a land of grain and new wine, a land of bread and vineyards.

Isa. 40:31 - Yet those who wait for the Lord Will gain new strength; They will mount up with wings like eagles, They will run and not get tired, They will walk and not become weary.

Isa. 41:1 - Coastlands, listen to Me in silence, And let the peoples gain new strength; Let them come forward, then let them speak; Let us come together for judgment.

Isa. 41:15 - Behold, I have made you a new, sharp threshing sledge with double edges; You will thresh the mountains and pulverize them, And will make the hills like chaff.

Isa. 42:9 - Behold, the former things have come to pass, Now I declare new things; Before they spring forth I proclaim them to you.

Isa. 42:10 - Sing to the Lord a new song, Sing His praise from the end of the earth! You who go down to the sea, and all that is in it. You islands, and those who dwell on them.

Isa. 43:19 - Behold, I will do something new, Now it will spring forth; Will you not be aware of it? I will even make a roadway in the wilderness, Rivers in the desert.

Isa. 47:13 - You are wearied with your many counsels; Let now the astrologers, Those who prophesy by the stars, Those who predict by the new moons, Stand up and save you from what will come upon you.

Isa. 48:6 - You have heard; look at all this. And you, will you not declare it? I proclaim to you new things from this time, Even hidden things which you have not known.

Isa. 62:2 - The nations will see your righteousness, And all kings your glory; And you will be called by a new name Which the mouth of the Lord will designate.

Isa. 62:8 - The Lord has sworn by His right hand and by His strong arm, "I will never again give your grain as food for your enemies; Nor will foreigners drink your new wine for which you have labored."

Isa. 65:8 - Thus says the Lord, "As the new wine is found in the cluster, And one says, 'Do not destroy it, for there is benefit in it,' So I will act on behalf of My servants In order not to destroy all of them."

Isa. 65:17 - For behold, I create new heavens and a new earth; And the former things will not be remembered or come to mind.

Isa. 66:14 - Then you will see this, and your heart will be glad, And your bones will flourish like the new grass; And the hand of the Lord will be made known to His servants, But He will be indignant toward His enemies.

Isa. 66:22 – "For just as the new heavens and the new earth Which I make will endure before Me," declares the Lord, "So your offspring and your name will endure."

Isa. 66:23 – "And it shall be from new moon to new moon And from sabbath to sabbath, All mankind will come to bow down before Me," says the Lord.

OBEYS

Isa. 50:10 - Who is among you that fears the Lord, That obeys the voice of His servant, That walks in darkness and has no light? Let him trust in the name of the Lord and rely on his God.

OBSTINATE

Isa. 48:4 - Because I know that you are obstinate, And your neck is an iron sinew And your forehead bronze.

OPEN

Isa. 22:22 - Then I will set the key of the house of David on his shoulder, When he opens no one will shut, When he shuts no one will open.

Isa. 26:2 - Open the gates, that the righteous nation may enter, The one that remains faithful.

Isa. 37:17 - Incline Your ear, O Lord, and hear; open Your eyes, O Lord, and see; and listen to all the words of Sennacherib, who sent them to reproach the living God.

Isa. 41:18 - I will open rivers on the bare heights And springs in the midst of the valleys; I will make the wilderness a pool of water And the dry land fountains of water.

Isa. 42:7 - To open blind eyes, To bring out prisoners from the dungeon And those who dwell in darkness from the prison.

Isa. 42:20 - You have seen many things, but you do not observe them; Your ears are open, but none hears.

Isa. 45:1 - Thus says the Lord to Cyrus His anointed, Whom I have taken by the right hand, To subdue nations before him And to loose the loins of kings; To open doors before him so that gates will not be shut.

Isa. 45:8 - Drip down, O heavens, from above, And let the clouds pour down righteousness; Let the earth open up and salvation bear fruit, And righteousness spring up with it. I, the Lord, have created it.

Isa. 48:8 - You have not heard, you have not known. Even from long ago your ear has not been open, Because I knew that you would deal very treacherously; And you have been called a rebel from birth.

Isa. 53:7 - He was oppressed and He was afflicted, Yet He did not open His mouth; Like a lamb that is led to slaughter, And like a sheep that is silent before its shearers, So He did not open His mouth.

Isa. 57:4 - Against whom do you jest? Against whom do you open wide your mouth And stick out your tongue? Are you not children of rebellion, Offspring of deceit.

Isa. 60:11 - Your gates will be open continually; They will not be closed day or night, So that men may bring to you the wealth of the nations, With their kings led in procession.

OPPRESSION

Isa. 30:12 - Therefore thus says the Holy One of Israel, "Since you have rejected this word And have put your trust in oppression and guile, and have relied on them."

Isa. 30:20 - Although the Lord has given you bread of privation and water of oppression, He, your Teacher will no longer hide Himself, but your eyes will behold your Teacher.

Isa. 53:8 - By oppression and judgment He was taken away; And as for His generation, who considered That He was cut off out of the land of the living For the transgression of my people, to whom the stroke was due?

Isa. 54:14 - In righteousness you will be established; You will be far from oppression, for you will not fear; And from terror, for it will not come near you.

Isa. 59:13 - Transgressing and denying the Lord, And turning away from our God, Speaking oppression and revolt, Conceiving in and uttering from the heart lying words.

OVERCOME

Isa. 28:1 - Woe to the proud crown of the drunkards of Ephraim, And to the fading flower of its glorious beauty, Which is at the head of the fertile valley Of those who are overcome with wine!

PAY

Isa. 5:12 - Their banquets are accompanied by lyre and harp, by tambourine and flute, and by wine; But they do not pay attention to the deeds of the Lord, Nor do they consider the work of His hands.

Isa. 10:30 - Cry aloud with your voice, O daughter of Gallim! Pay attention, Laishah and wretched Anathoth!

Isa. 21:7 - When he sees riders, horsemen in pairs, A train of donkeys, a train of camels, Let him pay close attention, very close attention.

Isa. 49:1 - Listen to Me, O islands, And pay attention, you peoples from afar. The Lord called Me from the womb; From the body of My mother He named Me.

Isa. 51:4 - Pay attention to Me, O My people, And give ear to Me, O My nation; For a law will go forth from Me, And I will set My justice for a light of the peoples.

PEACE

Isa. 9:6 - For a child will be born to us, a son will be given to us; And the government will rest on His shoulders; And His name will be called Wonderful Counselor, Mighty God, Eternal Father, Prince of Peace.

Isa. 9:7 - There will be no end to the increase of His government or of peace, On the throne of David and over his kingdom, To establish it and to uphold it with justice and righteousness From then on and forevermore. The zeal of the Lord of hosts will accomplish this.

Isa. 26:3 - The steadfast of mind You will keep in perfect peace, Because he trusts in You.

Isa. 26:12 - Lord, You will establish peace for us, Since You have also performed for us all our works.

Isa. 27:5 - Or let him rely on My protection, Let him make peace with Me, Let him make peace with Me.

Isa. 32:17 - And the work of righteousness will be peace, And the service of righteousness, quietness and confidence forever.

Isa. 33:7 - Behold, their brave men cry in the streets, The ambassadors of peace weep bitterly.

Isa. 36:16 – "Do not listen to Hezekiah," for thus says the king of Assyria, "Make your peace with me and come out to me, and eat each of his vine and each of his fig tree and drink each of the waters of his own cistern."

Isa. 39:8 - Then Hezekiah said to Isaiah, "The word of the Lord which you have spoken is good." For he thought, "For there will be peace and truth in my days."

Isa. 42:19 - Who is blind but My servant, Or so deaf as My messenger whom I send? Who is so blind as he that is at peace with Me, Or so blind as the servant of the Lord?

Isa. 48:22 – "There is no peace for the wicked," says the Lord.

Isa. 52:7 - How lovely on the mountains Are the feet of him who brings good news, Who announces peace And brings good news of happiness, Who announces salvation, And says to Zion, "Your God reigns!"

Isa. 54:10 – "For the mountains may be removed and the hills may shake, But My lovingkindness will not be removed from you, And My covenant of peace will not be shaken," Says the Lord who has compassion on you.

Isa. 55:12 - For you will go out with joy And be led forth with peace; The mountains and the hills will break forth into shouts of joy before you, And all the trees of the field will clap their hands.

Isa. 57:2 - He enters into peace; They rest in their beds, Each one who walked in his upright way.

Isa. 57:19 – "Creating the praise of the lips. Peace, peace to him who is far and to him who is near," Says the Lord, "and I will heal him."

Isa. 57:21 – "There is no peace," says my God, "for the wicked."

Isa. 59:8 - They do not know the way of peace, And there is no justice in their tracks; They have made their paths crooked, Whoever treads on them does not know peace.

Isa. 60:17 - Instead of bronze I will bring gold, And instead of iron I will bring silver, And instead of wood, bronze, And instead of stones, iron. And I will make peace your administrators And righteousness your overseers.

Isa. 66:12 - For thus says the Lord, "Behold, I extend peace to her like a river, And the glory of the nations like an overflowing stream; And you will be nursed, you will be carried on the hip and fondled on the knees."

PEGS

Isa. 54:2 - Enlarge the place of your tent; Stretch out the curtains of your dwellings, spare not; Lengthen your cords And strengthen your pegs.

PRAISE

Isa. 12:5 - Praise the Lord in song, for He has done excellent things; Let this be known throughout the earth.

Isa. 38:18 - For Sheol cannot thank You, Death cannot praise You; Those who go down to the pit cannot hope for Your faithfulness.

Isa. 42:8 - I am the Lord, that is My name; I will not give My glory to another, Nor My praise to graven images.

Isa. 42:10 - Sing to the Lord a new song, Sing His praise from the end of the earth! You who go down to the sea, and all that is in it. You islands, and those who dwell on them.

Isa. 42:12 - Let them give glory to the Lord And declare His praise in the coastlands.

Isa. 43:21 - The people whom I formed for Myself Will declare My praise.

Isa. 48:9 - For the sake of My name I delay My wrath, And for My praise I restrain it for you, In order not to cut you off.

Isa. 57:19 – "Creating the praise of the lips. Peace, peace to him who is far and to him who is near," Says the Lord, "and I will heal him."

Isa. 60:18 - Violence will not be heard again in your land, Nor devastation or destruction within your borders; But you will call your walls salvation, and your gates praise.

Isa. 61:3 - To grant those who mourn in Zion, Giving them a garland instead of ashes, The oil of gladness instead of mourning, The mantle of praise instead of a spirit of fainting. So they will be called oaks of righteousness, The planting of the Lord, that He may be glorified.

Isa. 61:11 - For as the earth brings forth its sprouts, And as a garden causes the things sown in it to spring up, So the Lord God will cause righteousness and praise To spring up before all the nations.

Isa. 62:7 - And give Him no rest until He establishes And makes Jerusalem a praise in the earth.

Isa. 62:9 - But those who garner it will eat it and praise the Lord; And those who gather it will drink it in the courts of My sanctuary.

PRESENCE

Isa. 1:7 - Your land is desolate, Your cities are burned with fire, Your fields — strangers are devouring them in your presence; It is desolation, as overthrown by strangers.

Isa. 3:8 - For Jerusalem has stumbled and Judah has fallen, Because their speech and their actions are against the Lord, To rebel against His glorious presence.

Isa. 9:3 - You shall multiply the nation, You shall increase their gladness; They will be glad in Your presence As with the gladness of harvest, As men rejoice when they divide the spoil.

Isa. 19:1 - The oracle concerning Egypt. Behold, the Lord is riding on a swift cloud and is about to come to Egypt; The idols of Egypt will tremble at His presence, And the heart of the Egyptians will melt within them.

Isa. 23:18 - Her gain and her harlot's wages will be set apart to the Lord; it will not be stored up or hoarded, but her gain will become sufficient food and choice attire for those who dwell in the presence of the Lord.

Isa. 48:19 - Your descendants would have been like the sand, And your offspring like its grains; Their name would never be cut off or destroyed from My presence.

Isa. 63:9 - In all their affliction He was afflicted, And the angel of His presence saved them; In His love and in His mercy He redeemed them, And He lifted them and carried them all the days of old.

Isa. 64:1 - Oh, that You would rend the heavens and come down, That the mountains might quake at Your presence.

Isa. 64:2 - As fire kindles the brushwood, as fire causes water to boil— To make Your name known to Your adversaries, That the nations may tremble at Your presence!

Isa. 64:3 - When You did awesome things which we did not expect, You came down, the mountains quaked at Your presence.

PRIDE

Isa. 2:17 - The pride of man will be humbled And the loftiness of men will be abased; And the Lord alone will be exalted in that day.

Isa. 4:2 - In that day the Branch of the Lord will be beautiful and glorious, and the fruit of the earth will be the pride and the adornment of the survivors of Israel.

Isa. 9:9 - And all the people know it, That is, Ephraim and the inhabitants of Samaria, Asserting in pride and in arrogance of heart.

Isa. 13:19 - And Babylon, the beauty of kingdoms, the glory of the Chaldeans' pride, Will be as when God overthrew Sodom and Gomorrah.

Isa. 16:6 - We have heard of the pride of Moab, an excessive pride; Even of his arrogance, pride, and fury; His idle boasts are false.

Isa. 23:9 - The Lord of hosts has planned it, to defile the pride of all beauty, To despise all the honored of the earth.

Isa. 25:11 - And he will spread out his hands in the middle of it As a swimmer spreads out his hands to swim, But the Lord will lay low his pride together with the trickery of his hands.

Isa. 60:15 - Whereas you have been forsaken and hated With no one passing through, I will make you an everlasting pride, A joy from generation to generation.

PRINCE

Isa. 9:6 - For a child will be born to us, a son will be given to us; And the government will rest on His shoulders; And His name will be called Wonderful Counselor, Mighty God, Eternal Father, Prince of Peace.

PROCLAIM

Isa. 34:12 - Its nobles—there is no one there Whom they may proclaim king— And all its princes will be nothing.

Isa. 42:9 - Behold, the former things have come to pass, Now I declare new things; Before they spring forth I proclaim them to you.

Isa. 43:9 - All the nations have gathered together So that the peoples may be assembled. Who among them can declare this And proclaim to us the former things? Let them present their witnesses that they may be justified, Or let them hear and say, "It is true."

Isa. 44:7 - Who is like Me? Let him proclaim and declare it; Yes, let him recount it to Me in order, From the time that I established the ancient nation. And let them declare to them the things that are coming And the events that are going to take place.

Isa. 48:6 - You have heard; look at all this. And you, will you not declare it? I proclaim to you new things from this time, Even hidden things which you have not known.

Isa. 48:20 - Go forth from Babylon! Flee from the Chaldeans! Declare with the sound of joyful shouting, proclaim this, Send it out to the end of the earth; Say, "The Lord has redeemed His servant Jacob."

Isa. 61:1 - The Spirit of the Lord God is upon me, Because the Lord has anointed me To bring good news to the afflicted; He has sent me to bind up the brokenhearted, To proclaim liberty to captives And freedom to prisoners.

Isa. 61:2 - To proclaim the favorable year of the Lord And the day of vengeance of our God; To comfort all who mourn.

PUNISHMENT

Isa. 10:3 - Now what will you do in the day of punishment, And in the devastation which will come from afar? To whom will you flee for help? And where will you leave your wealth?

Isa. 30:32 - And every blow of the rod of punishment, Which the Lord will lay on him, Will be with the music of tambourines and lyres; And in battles, brandishing weapons, He will fight them.

RADIANT

Isa. 60:5 - Then you shall see and become radiant, And your heart shall swell with joy; Because the abundance of the sea shall be turned to you, The wealth of the Gentiles shall come to you.[2]

REDEEMED

Isa. 1:27 - Zion shall be redeemed with justice, And her penitents with righteousness.

Isa. 29:22 - Therefore thus says the Lord, who redeemed Abraham, concerning the house of Jacob: "Jacob shall not now be ashamed, Nor shall his face now grow pale."

Isa. 35:9 - No lion shall be there, Nor shall any ravenous beast go up on it; It shall not be found there. But the redeemed shall walk there.

Isa. 43:1 - But now, thus says the Lord, who created you, O Jacob, And He who formed you, O Israel: "Fear not, for I have redeemed you; I have called you by your name; You are Mine."

Isa. 44:22 - I have blotted out, like a thick cloud, your transgressions, And like a cloud, your sins. Return to Me, for I have redeemed you.

---

[2] From this point forward all Scripture quotations, unless otherwise noted, are from the *New King James Version*.

Isa. 44:23 - Sing, O heavens, for the Lord has done it! Shout, you lower parts of the earth; Break forth into singing, you mountains, O forest, and every tree in it! For the Lord has redeemed Jacob, And glorified Himself in Israel.

Isa. 48:20 - Go forth from Babylon! Flee from the Chaldeans! With a voice of singing, Declare, proclaim this, Utter it to the end of the earth; Say, "The Lord has redeemed His servant Jacob!"

Isa. 51:10 - Are You not the One who dried up the sea, The waters of the great deep; That made the depths of the sea a road For the redeemed to cross over?

Isa. 52:3 - For thus says the Lord: "You have sold yourselves for nothing, And you shall be redeemed without money."

Isa. 52:9 - Break forth into joy, sing together, You waste places of Jerusalem! For the Lord has comforted His people, He has redeemed Jerusalem.

Isa. 62:12 - And they shall call them The Holy People, The Redeemed of the Lord; And you shall be called Sought Out, A City Not Forsaken.

Isa. 63:4 - For the day of vengeance is in My heart, And the year of My redeemed has come.

Isa. 63:9 - In all their affliction He was afflicted, And the Angel of His Presence saved them; In His love and in His pity He redeemed them; And He bore them and carried them All the days of old.

RELY

Isa. 30:12 - Therefore thus says the Holy One of Israel: "Because you despise this word, And trust in oppression and perversity, And rely on them."

Isa. 31:1 - Woe to those who go down to Egypt for help, And rely on horses, Who trust in chariots because they are many, And in horsemen because they are very strong, But who do not look to the Holy One of Israel, Nor seek the Lord!

Isa. 50:10 - Who among you fears the Lord? Who obeys the voice of His Servant? Who walks in darkness And has no light? Let him trust in the name of the Lord And rely upon his God.

REMNANT

Isa. 1:9 - Unless the Lord of hosts Had left to us a very small remnant, We would have become like Sodom, We would have been made like Gomorrah.

Isa. 10:20 - And it shall come to pass in that day That the remnant of Israel, And such as have escaped of the house of Jacob, Will never again depend on him who defeated them, But will depend on the Lord, the Holy One of Israel, in truth.

Isa. 10:21 - The remnant will return, the remnant of Jacob, To the Mighty God.

Isa. 10:22 - For though your people, O Israel, be as the sand of the sea, A remnant of them will return; The destruction decreed shall overflow with righteousness.

Isa. 11:11 - It shall come to pass in that day That the Lord shall set His hand again the second time To recover the remnant of His people who are left, From Assyria and Egypt, From Pathros and Cush, From Elam and Shinar, From Hamath and the islands of the sea.

Isa. 11:16 - There will be a highway for the remnant of His people Who will be left from Assyria, As it was for Israel In the day that he came up from the land of Egypt.

Isa. 14:22 – "For I will rise up against them," says the Lord of hosts, "And cut off from Babylon the name and remnant, And offspring and posterity," says the Lord.

Isa. 14:30 - The firstborn of the poor will feed, And the needy will lie down in safety; I will kill your roots with famine, And it will slay your remnant.

Isa. 15:9 - For the waters of Dimon will be full of blood; Because I will bring more upon Dimon, Lions upon him who escapes from Moab, And on the remnant of the land.

Isa. 16:14 - But now the Lord has spoken, saying, "Within three years, as the years of a hired man, the glory of Moab will be despised with all that great multitude, and the remnant will be very small and feeble."

Isa. 17:3 – "The fortress also will cease from Ephraim, The kingdom from Damascus, And the remnant of Syria; They will be as the glory of the children of Israel," Says the Lord of hosts.

Isa. 28:5 - In that day the Lord of hosts will be For a crown of glory and a diadem of beauty To the remnant of His people.

Isa. 37:4 - It may be that the Lord your God will hear the words of the Rabshakeh, whom his master the king of Assyria has sent to reproach the living God, and will rebuke the words which the Lord your God has heard. Therefore lift up your prayer for the remnant that is left.

Isa. 37:31 - And the remnant who have escaped of the house of Judah Shall again take root downward, And bear fruit upward.

Isa. 37:32 - For out of Jerusalem shall go a remnant, And those who escape from Mount Zion. The zeal of the Lord of hosts will do this.

Isa. 46:3 - Listen to Me, O house of Jacob, And all the remnant of the house of Israel, Who have been upheld by Me from birth, Who have been carried from the womb.

REND

Isa. 64:1 - Oh, that You would rend the heavens! That You would come down! That the mountains might shake at Your presence.

REST

Isa. 7:19 - They will come, and all of them will rest In the desolate valleys and in the clefts of the rocks, And on all thorns and in all pastures.

Isa. 10:19 Then the rest of the trees of his forest Will be so few in number That a child may write them.

Isa. 11:2 - The Spirit of the Lord shall rest upon Him, The Spirit of wisdom and understanding, The Spirit of counsel and might, The Spirit of knowledge and of the fear of the Lord.

Isa. 14:3 - It shall come to pass in the day the Lord gives you rest from your sorrow, and from your fear and the hard bondage in which you were made to serve.

Isa. 14:7 - The whole earth is at rest and quiet; They break forth into singing.

Isa. 18:4 - For so the Lord said to me, "I will take My rest, And I will look from My dwelling place Like clear heat in sunshine, Like a cloud of dew in the heat of harvest."

Isa. 23:12 - And He said, "You will rejoice no more, O you oppressed virgin daughter of Sidon. Arise, cross over to Cyprus; There also you will have no rest."

Isa. 25:10 - For on this mountain the hand of the Lord will rest, And Moab shall be trampled down under Him, As straw is trampled down for the refuse heap.

Isa. 28:12 - To whom He said, "This is the rest with which You may cause the weary to rest," And, "This is the refreshing"; Yet they would not hear.

Isa. 30:15 - For thus says the Lord God, the Holy One of Israel: "In returning and rest you shall be saved; In quietness and confidence shall be your strength." But you would not.

Isa. 34:14 - The wild beasts of the desert shall also meet with the jackals, And the wild goat shall bleat to its companion; Also the night creature shall rest there, And find for herself a place of rest.

Isa. 44:17 - And the rest of it he makes into a god, His carved image. He falls down before it and worships it, Prays to it and says, "Deliver me, for you are my god!"

Isa. 44:19 - And no one considers in his heart, Nor is there knowledge nor understanding to say, "I have burned half of it in the fire, Yes, I have also baked bread on its coals; I have roasted meat and eaten it; And shall I make the rest of it an abomination? Shall I fall down before a block of wood?"

Isa. 51:4 - Listen to Me, My people; And give ear to Me, O My nation: For law will proceed from Me, And I will make My justice rest As a light of the peoples.

Isa. 57:2 - He shall enter into peace; They shall rest in their beds, Each one walking in his uprightness.

Isa. 57:20 - But the wicked are like the troubled sea, When it cannot rest, Whose waters cast up mire and dirt.

Isa. 62:1 - For Zion's sake I will not hold My peace, And for Jerusalem's sake I will not rest, Until her righteousness goes forth as brightness, And her salvation as a lamp that burns.

Isa. 62:7 - And give Him no rest till He establishes And till He makes Jerusalem a praise in the earth.

Isa. 63:14 - As a beast goes down into the valley, And the Spirit of the Lord causes him to rest, So You lead Your people, To make Yourself a glorious name.

Isa. 66:1 - Thus says the Lord: "Heaven is My throne, And earth is My footstool. Where is the house that you will build Me? And where is the place of My rest?"

RESTORE

Isa. 1:26 - I will restore your judges as at the first, And your counselors as at the beginning. Afterward you shall be called the city of righteousness, the faithful city.

Isa. 38:16 - O Lord, by these things men live; And in all these things is the life of my spirit; So You will restore me and make me live.

Isa. 42:22 - But this is a people robbed and plundered; All of them are snared in holes, And they are hidden in prison houses; They are for prey, and no one delivers; For plunder, and no one says, "Restore!"

Isa. 49:6 - Indeed He says, "It is too small a thing that You should be My Servant To raise up the tribes of Jacob, And to restore the preserved ones of Israel; I will also give You as a light to the Gentiles, That You should be My salvation to the ends of the earth.'"

Isa. 49:8 - Thus says the Lord: "In an acceptable time I have heard You, And in the day of salvation I have helped You; I will preserve You and give You As a covenant to the people, To restore the earth, To cause them to inherit the desolate heritages."

Isa. 57:18 - I have seen his ways, and will heal him; I will also lead him, And restore comforts to him And to his mourners.

ROOT

Isa. 5:24 - Therefore, as the fire devours the stubble, And the flame consumes the chaff, So their root will be as rottenness, And their blossom will ascend like dust;

Because they have rejected the law of the Lord of hosts, And despised the word of the Holy One of Israel.

Isa. 11:10 - And in that day there shall be a Root of Jesse, Who shall stand as a banner to the people; For the Gentiles shall seek Him, And His resting place shall be glorious.

Isa. 27:6 - Those who come He shall cause to take root in Jacob; Israel shall blossom and bud, And fill the face of the world with fruit.

Isa. 37:31 - And the remnant who have escaped of the house of Judah Shall again take root downward, And bear fruit upward.

Isa. 40:24 - Scarcely shall they be planted, Scarcely shall they be sown, Scarcely shall their stock take root in the earth, When He will also blow on them, And they will wither, And the whirlwind will take them away like stubble.

Isa. 53:2 - For He shall grow up before Him as a tender plant, And as a root out of dry ground. He has no form or comeliness; And when we see Him, There is no beauty that we should desire Him.

SALVATION

Isa. 12:2 - Behold, God is my salvation, I will trust and not be afraid; -'For YAH, the Lord, is my strength and song; He also has become my salvation.

Isa. 12:3 - Therefore with joy you will draw water From the wells of salvation.

Isa. 17:10 - Because you have forgotten the God of your salvation, And have not been mindful of the Rock of your stronghold, Therefore you will plant pleasant plants And set out foreign seedlings.

Isa. 25:9 - And it will be said in that day: "Behold, this is our God; We have waited for Him, and He will save us. This is the Lord; We have waited for Him; We will be glad and rejoice in His salvation."

Isa. 26:1 - In that day this song will be sung in the land of Judah: We have a strong city; God will appoint salvation for walls and bulwarks.

Isa. 33:2 - O Lord, be gracious to us; We have waited for You. Be their arm every morning, Our salvation also in the time of trouble.

Isa. 33:6 - Wisdom and knowledge will be the stability of your times, And the strength of salvation; The fear of the Lord is His treasure.

Isa. 45:8 - Rain down, you heavens, from above, And let the skies pour down righteousness; Let the earth open, let them bring forth salvation, And let righteousness spring up together. I, the Lord, have created it.

Isa. 45:17 - But Israel shall be saved by the Lord With an everlasting salvation; You shall not be ashamed or disgraced Forever and ever.

Isa. 46:13 I bring My righteousness near, it shall not be far off; My salvation shall not linger. And I will place salvation in Zion, For Israel My glory.

Isa. 49:6 - Indeed He says, "It is too small a thing that You should be My Servant To raise up the tribes of Jacob, And to restore the preserved ones of Israel; I will also give You as a light to the Gentiles, That You should be My salvation to the ends of the earth."

Isa. 49:8 - Thus says the Lord: "In an acceptable time I have heard You, And in the day of salvation I have helped You; I will preserve You and give You As a covenant to the people, To restore the earth, To cause them to inherit the desolate heritages."

Isa. 51:5 - My righteousness is near, My salvation has gone forth, And My arms will judge the peoples; The coastlands will wait upon Me, And on My arm they will trust.

Isa. 51:6 - Lift up your eyes to the heavens, And look on the earth beneath. For the heavens will vanish away like smoke, The earth will grow old like a garment, And those who dwell in it will die in like manner; But My salvation will be forever, And My righteousness will not be abolished.

Isa. 51:8 - For the moth will eat them up like a garment, And the worm will eat them like wool; But My righteousness will be forever, And My salvation from generation to generation.

Isa. 52:7 - How beautiful upon the mountains Are the feet of him who brings good news, Who proclaims peace, Who brings glad tidings of good things, Who proclaims salvation, Who says to Zion, "Your God reigns!"

Isa. 52:10 - The Lord has made bare His holy arm In the eyes of all the nations; And all the ends of the earth shall see The salvation of our God.

Isa. 56:1 - Thus says the Lord: "Keep justice, and do righteousness, For My salvation is about to come, And My righteousness to be revealed."

Isa. 59:11 - We all growl like bears, And moan sadly like doves; We look for justice, but there is none; For salvation, but it is far from us.

Isa. 59:16 - He saw that there was no man, And wondered that there was no intercessor; Therefore His own arm brought salvation for Him; And His own righteousness, it sustained Him.

Isa. 59:17 - For He put on righteousness as a breastplate, And a helmet of salvation on His head; He put on the garments of vengeance for clothing, And was clad with zeal as a cloak.

Isa. 60:18 - Violence shall no longer be heard in your land, Neither wasting nor destruction within your borders; But you shall call your walls Salvation, And your gates Praise.

Isa. 61:10 - I will greatly rejoice in the Lord, My soul shall be joyful in my God; For He has clothed me with the garments of salvation, He has covered me with the robe of righteousness, As a bridegroom decks himself with ornaments, And as a bride adorns herself with her jewels.

Isa. 62:1 - For Zion's sake I will not hold My peace, And for Jerusalem's sake I will not rest, Until her righteousness goes forth as brightness, And her salvation as a lamp that burns.

Isa. 62:11 - Indeed the Lord has proclaimed To the end of the world: "Say to the daughter of Zion, 'Surely your salvation is coming; Behold, His reward is with Him, And His work before Him.'"

Isa. 63:5 - I looked, but there was no one to help, And I wondered That there was no one to uphold; Therefore My own arm brought salvation for Me; And My own fury, it sustained Me.

SAVE

Isa. 25:9 - And it will be said in that day: "Behold, this is our God; We have waited for Him, and He will save us. This is the Lord; We have waited for Him; We will be glad and rejoice in His salvation."

Isa. 33:22 - (For the Lord is our Judge, The Lord is our Lawgiver, The Lord is our King; He will save us).

Isa. 35:4 - Say to those who are fearful-hearted, "Be strong, do not fear! Behold, your God will come with vengeance, With the recompense of God; He will come and save you."

Isa. 37:20 - Now therefore, O Lord our God, save us from his hand, that all the kingdoms of the earth may know that You are the Lord, You alone.

Isa. 37:35 - For I will defend this city, to save it For My own sake and for My servant David's sake.

Isa. 38:20 - The Lord was ready to save me; Therefore we will sing my songs with stringed instruments All the days of our life, in the house of the Lord.

Isa. 45:20 - Assemble yourselves and come; Draw near together, You who have escaped from the nations. They have no knowledge, Who carry the wood of their carved image, And pray to a god that cannot save.

Isa. 46:7 - They bear it on the shoulder, they carry it And set it in its place, and it stands; From its place it shall not move. Though one cries out to it, yet it cannot answer Nor save him out of his trouble.

Isa. 47:13 - You are wearied in the multitude of your counsels; Let now the astrologers, the stargazers, And the monthly prognosticators Stand up and save you From what shall come upon you.

Isa. 47:15 - Thus shall they be to you With whom you have labored, Your merchants from your youth; They shall wander each one to his quarter. No one shall save you.

Isa. 49:25 - But thus says the Lord: "Even the captives of the mighty shall be taken away, And the prey of the terrible be delivered; For I will contend with him who contends with you, And I will save your children.

Isa. 59:1 - Behold, the Lord's hand is not shortened, That it cannot save; Nor His ear heavy, That it cannot hear.

Isa. 63:1 - Who is this who comes from Edom, With dyed garments from Bozrah, This One who is glorious in His apparel, Traveling in the greatness of His strength? —"I who speak in righteousness, mighty to save."

SAVIOR

Isa. 19:20 - And it will be for a sign and for a witness to the Lord of hosts in the land of Egypt; for they will cry to the Lord because of the oppressors, and He will send them a Savior and a Mighty One, and He will deliver them.

Isa. 43:3 - For I am the Lord your God, The Holy One of Israel, your Savior; I gave Egypt for your ransom, Ethiopia and Seba in your place.

Isa. 43:11 - I, even I, am the Lord, And besides Me there is no savior.

Isa. 45:15 - Truly You are God, who hide Yourself, O God of Israel, the Savior!

Isa. 45:21 - Tell and bring forth your case; Yes, let them take counsel together. Who has declared this from ancient time? Who has told it from that time? Have not I, the Lord? And there is no other God besides Me, A just God and a Savior; There is none besides Me.

Isa. 49:26 - I will feed those who oppress you with their own flesh, And they shall be drunk with their own blood as with sweet wine. All flesh shall know That I, the Lord, am your Savior, And your Redeemer, the Mighty One of Jacob.

Isa. 60:16 - You shall drink the milk of the Gentiles, And milk the breast of kings; You shall know that I, the Lord, am your Savior And your Redeemer, the Mighty One of Jacob.

Isa. 63:8 - For He said, "Surely they are My people, Children who will not lie." So He became their Savior.

SEND

Isa. 6:8 - Also I heard the voice of the Lord, saying: "Whom shall I send, And who will go for Us?" Then I said, "Here am I! Send me."

Isa. 10:6 - I will send him against an ungodly nation, And against the people of My wrath I will give him charge, To seize the spoil, to take the prey, And to tread them down like the mire of the streets.

Isa. 10:16 - Therefore the Lord, the Lord of hosts, Will send leanness among his fat ones; And under his glory He will kindle a burning Like the burning of a fire.

Isa. 16:1 - Send the lamb to the ruler of the land, From Sela to the wilderness, To the mount of the daughter of Zion.

Isa. 19:20 - And it will be for a sign and for a witness to the Lord of hosts in the land of Egypt; for they will cry to the Lord because of the oppressors, and He will send them a Savior and a Mighty One, and He will deliver them.

Isa. 32:20 - Blessed are you who sow beside all waters, Who send out freely the feet of the ox and the donkey.

Isa. 37:7 - Surely I will send a spirit upon him, and he shall hear a rumor and return to his own land; and I will cause him to fall by the sword in his own land.

Isa. 42:19 - Who is blind but My servant, Or deaf as My messenger whom I send? Who is blind as he who is perfect, And blind as the Lord's servant?

Isa. 43:14 - Thus says the Lord, your Redeemer, The Holy One of Israel: "For your sake I will send to Babylon, And bring them all down as fugitives — The Chaldeans, who rejoice in their ships."

Isa. 66:19 - I will set a sign among them; and those among them who escape I will send to the nations: to Tarshish and Pul and Lud, who draw the bow, and Tubal and Javan, to the coastlands afar off who have not heard My fame nor seen My glory. And they shall declare My glory among the Gentiles.

SERVANT

Isa. 20:3 - Then the Lord said, "Just as My servant Isaiah has walked naked and barefoot three years for a sign and a wonder against Egypt and Ethiopia."

Isa. 22:20 - Then it shall be in that day, That I will call My servant Eliakim the son of Hilkiah.

Isa. 24:2 - And it shall be: As with the people, so with the priest; As with the servant, so with his master; As with the maid, so with her mistress; As with the buyer, so with the seller; As with the lender, so with the borrower; As with the creditor, so with the debtor.

Isa. 37:35 - For I will defend this city, to save it For My own sake and for My servant David's sake.

Isa. 41:8 - But you, Israel, are My servant, Jacob whom I have chosen, The descendants of Abraham My friend.

Isa. 41:9 - You whom I have taken from the ends of the earth, And called from its farthest regions, And said to you, "You are My servant, I have chosen you and have not cast you away."

Isa. 42:1 - Behold! My Servant whom I uphold, My Elect One in whom My soul delights! I have put My Spirit upon Him; He will bring forth justice to the Gentiles.

Isa. 42:19 - Who is blind but My servant, Or deaf as My messenger whom I send? Who is blind as he who is perfect, And blind as the Lord's servant?

Isa. 43:10 – "You are My witnesses," says the Lord, "And My servant whom I have chosen, That you may know and believe Me, And understand that I am He. Before Me there was no God formed, Nor shall there be after Me."

Isa. 44:1 - Yet hear now, O Jacob My servant, And Israel whom I have chosen.

Isa. 44:2 - Thus says the Lord who made you And formed you from the womb, who will help you: 'Fear not, O Jacob My servant; And you, Jeshurun, whom I have chosen.

Isa. 44:21 - Remember these, O Jacob, And Israel, for you are My servant; I have formed you, you are My servant; O Israel, you will not be forgotten by Me!

Isa. 44:26 - Who confirms the word of His servant, And performs the counsel of His messengers; Who says to Jerusalem, "You shall be inhabited," To the cities of Judah, "You shall be built," And I will raise up her waste places.

Isa. 45:4 - For Jacob My servant's sake, And Israel My elect, I have even called you by your name; I have named you, though you have not known Me.

Isa. 48:20 - Go forth from Babylon! Flee from the Chaldeans! With a voice of singing, Declare, proclaim this, Utter it to the end of the earth; Say, "The Lord has redeemed His servant Jacob!"

Isa. 49:3 - And He said to me, "You are My servant, O Israel, In whom I will be glorified."

Isa. 49:5 - And now the Lord says, Who formed Me from the womb to be His Servant, To bring Jacob back to Him, So that Israel is gathered to Him (For I shall be glorious in the eyes of the Lord, And My God shall be My strength).

Isa. 49:6 - Indeed He says, "It is too small a thing that You should be My Servant To raise up the tribes of Jacob, And to restore the preserved ones of Israel; I will also give You as a light to the Gentiles, That You should be My salvation to the ends of the earth."

Isa. 49:7 - Thus says the Lord, The Redeemer of Israel, their Holy One, To Him whom man despises, To Him whom the nation abhors, To the Servant of rulers: "Kings shall see and arise, Princes also shall worship, Because of the Lord who is faithful, The Holy One of Israel; And He has chosen You."

Isa. 50:10 - Who among you fears the Lord? Who obeys the voice of His Servant? Who walks in darkness And has no light? Let him trust in the name of the Lord And rely upon his God.

Isa. 52:13 - Behold, My Servant shall deal prudently; He shall be exalted and extolled and be very high.

Isa. 53:11 - He shall see the labor of His soul, and be satisfied. By His knowledge My righteous Servant shall justify many, For He shall bear their iniquities.

SHAKE

Isa. 2:19 - They shall go into the holes of the rocks, And into the caves of the earth, From the terror of the Lord And the glory of His majesty, When He arises to shake the earth mightily.

Isa. 2:21 - To go into the clefts of the rocks, And into the crags of the rugged rocks, From the terror of the Lord And the glory of His majesty, When He arises to shake the earth mightily.

Isa. 10:32 - As yet he will remain at Nob that day; He will shake his fist at the mount of the daughter of Zion, The hill of Jerusalem.

Isa. 11:15 - The Lord will utterly destroy the tongue of the Sea of Egypt; With His mighty wind He will shake His fist over the River, And strike it in the seven streams, And make men cross over dry-shod.

Isa. 13:13 - Therefore I will shake the heavens, And the earth will move out of her place, In the wrath of the Lord of hosts And in the day of His fierce anger.

Isa. 33:9 - The earth mourns and languishes, Lebanon is shamed and shriveled; Sharon is like a wilderness, And Bashan and Carmel shake off their fruits.

Isa. 52:2 - Shake yourself from the dust, arise; Sit down, O Jerusalem! Loose yourself from the bonds of your neck, O captive daughter of Zion!

Isa. 64:1 - Oh, that You would rend the heavens! That You would come down! That the mountains might shake at Your presence.

SHARE

Isa. 58:7 - Is it not to share your bread with the hungry, And that you bring to your house the poor who are cast out; When you see the naked, that you cover him, And not hide yourself from your own flesh?

SHINE

Isa. 13:10 - For the stars of heaven and their constellations Will not give their light; The sun will be darkened in its going forth, And the moon will not cause its light to shine.

Isa. 60:1 - Arise, shine; For your light has come! And the glory of the Lord is risen upon you.

SHOULDER

Isa. 9:4 - For You have broken the yoke of his burden And the staff of his shoulder, The rod of his oppressor, As in the day of Midian.

Isa. 9:6 - For unto us a Child is born, Unto us a Son is given; And the government will be upon His shoulder. And His name will be called Wonderful, Counselor, Mighty God, Everlasting Father, Prince of Peace.

Isa. 10:27 - It shall come to pass in that day That his burden will be taken away from your shoulder, And his yoke from your neck, And the yoke will be destroyed because of the anointing oil.

Isa. 11:14 - But they shall fly down upon the shoulder of the Philistines toward the west; Together they shall plunder the people of the East; They shall lay their hand on Edom and Moab; And the people of Ammon shall obey them.

Isa. 22:22 - The key of the house of David I will lay on his shoulder; So he shall open, and no one shall shut; And he shall shut, and no one shall open.

Isa. 46:7 - They bear it on the shoulder, they carry it And set it in its place, and it stands; From its place it shall not move. Though one cries out to it, yet it cannot answer Nor save him out of his trouble.

SHOUTING

Isa. 16:10 - Gladness is taken away, And joy from the plentiful field; In the vineyards there will be no singing, Nor will there be shouting; No treaders will tread out wine in the presses; I have made their shouting cease.

SHUT

Isa. 6:10 - Make the heart of this people dull, And their ears heavy, And shut their eyes; Lest they see with their eyes, And hear with their ears, And understand with their heart, And return and be healed.

Isa. 22:22 - The key of the house of David I will lay on his shoulder; So he shall open, and no one shall shut; And he shall shut, and no one shall open.

Isa. 24:10 - The city of confusion is broken down; Every house is shut up, so that none may go in.

Isa. 24:22 - They will be gathered together, As prisoners are gathered in the pit, And will be shut up in the prison; After many days they will be punished.

Isa. 26:20 - Come, my people, enter your chambers, And shut your doors behind you; Hide yourself, as it were, for a little moment, Until the indignation is past.

Isa. 44:18 - They do not know nor understand; For He has shut their eyes, so that they cannot see, And their hearts, so that they cannot understand.

Isa. 45:1 - Thus says the Lord to His anointed, To Cyrus, whose right hand I have held — To subdue nations before him And loose the armor of kings, To open before him the double doors, So that the gates will not be shut.

Isa. 52:15 - So shall He sprinkle many nations. Kings shall shut their mouths at Him; For what had not been told them they shall see, And what they had not heard they shall consider.

Isa. 60:11 - Therefore your gates shall be open continually; They shall not be shut day or night, That men may bring to you the wealth of the Gentiles, And their kings in procession.

Isa. 66:9 – "Shall I bring to the time of birth, and not cause delivery?" says the Lord. "Shall I who cause delivery shut up the womb?" says your God.

SIGN

Isa. 7:11 - Ask a sign for yourself from the Lord your God; ask it either in the depth or in the height above.

Isa. 7:14 - Therefore the Lord Himself will give you a sign: Behold, the virgin shall conceive and bear a Son, and shall call His name Immanuel.

Isa. 19:20 - And it will be for a sign and for a witness to the Lord of hosts in the land of Egypt; for they will cry to the Lord because of the oppressors, and He will send them a Savior and a Mighty One, and He will deliver them.

Isa. 20:3 - Then the Lord said, "Just as My servant Isaiah has walked naked and barefoot three years for a sign and a wonder against Egypt and Ethiopia."

Isa. 37:30 - This shall be a sign to you: You shall eat this year such as grows of itself, And the second year what springs from the same; Also in the third year sow and reap, Plant vineyards and eat the fruit of them.

Isa. 38:7 - And this is the sign to you from the Lord, that the Lord will do this thing which He has spoken.

Isa. 38:22 - And Hezekiah had said, "What is the sign that I shall go up to the house of the Lord?"

Isa. 55:13 - Instead of the thorn shall come up the cypress tree, And instead of the brier shall come up the myrtle tree; And it shall be to the Lord for a name, For an everlasting sign that shall not be cut off.

Isa. 66:19 - I will set a sign among them; and those among them who escape I will send to the nations: to Tarshish and Pul and Lud, who draw the bow, and Tubal and Javan, to the coastlands afar off who have not heard My fame nor seen My glory. And they shall declare My glory among the Gentiles.

SINFUL

Isa. 1:4 - Alas, sinful nation, A people laden with iniquity, A brood of evildoers, Children who are corrupters! They have forsaken the Lord, They have provoked to anger The Holy One of Israel, They have turned away backward.

SING

Isa. 5:1 - Now let me sing to my Well-beloved A song of my Beloved regarding His vineyard: My Well-beloved has a vineyard On a very fruitful hill.

Isa. 12:5 - Sing to the Lord, For He has done excellent things; This is known in all the earth.

Isa. 23:16 - Take a harp, go about the city, You forgotten harlot; Make sweet melody, sing many songs, That you may be remembered.

Isa. 24:14 - They shall lift up their voice, they shall sing; For the majesty of the Lord They shall cry aloud from the sea.

Isa. 26:19 - Your dead shall live; Together with my dead body they shall arise. Awake and sing, you who dwell in dust; For your dew is like the dew of herbs, And the earth shall cast out the dead.

Isa. 27:2 In that day sing to her, "A vineyard of red wine!"

Isa. 35:6 - Then the lame shall leap like a deer, And the tongue of the dumb sing. For waters shall burst forth in the wilderness, And streams in the desert.

Isa. 38:20 - The Lord was ready to save me; Therefore we will sing my songs with stringed instruments All the days of our life, in the house of the Lord.

Isa. 42:10 - Sing to the Lord a new song, And His praise from the ends of the earth, You who go down to the sea, and all that is in it, You coastlands and you inhabitants of them!

Isa. 42:11 - Let the wilderness and its cities lift up their voice, The villages that Kedar inhabits. Let the inhabitants of Sela sing, Let them shout from the top of the mountains.

Isa. 44:23 - Sing, O heavens, for the Lord has done it! Shout, you lower parts of the earth; Break forth into singing, you mountains, O forest, and every tree in it! For the Lord has redeemed Jacob, And glorified Himself in Israel.

Isa. 49:13 - Sing, O heavens! Be joyful, O earth! And break out in singing, O mountains! For the Lord has comforted His people, And will have mercy on His afflicted.

Isa. 52:8 - Your watchmen shall lift up their voices, With their voices they shall sing together; For they shall see eye to eye When the Lord brings back Zion.
Isa. 52:9 - Break forth into joy, sing together, You waste places of Jerusalem! For the Lord has comforted His people, He has redeemed Jerusalem.
Isa. 54:1 – "Sing, O barren, You who have not borne! Break forth into singing, and cry aloud, You who have not labored with child! For more are the children of the desolate Than the children of the married woman," says the Lord.
Isa. 65:14 - Behold, My servants shall sing for joy of heart, But you shall cry for sorrow of heart, And wail for grief of spirit.

SONG
Isa. 5:1 - Now let me sing to my Well-beloved A song of my Beloved regarding His vineyard: My Well-beloved has a vineyard On a very fruitful hill.
Isa. 12:2 - Behold, God is my salvation, I will trust and not be afraid; "For YAH, the Lord, is my strength and song; He also has become my salvation."
Isa. 23:15 - Now it shall come to pass in that day that Tyre will be forgotten seventy years, according to the days of one king. At the end of seventy years it will happen to Tyre as in the song of the harlot.
Isa. 24:9 - They shall not drink wine with a song; Strong drink is bitter to those who drink it.
Isa. 25:5 - You will reduce the noise of aliens, As heat in a dry place; As heat in the shadow of a cloud, The song of the terrible ones will be diminished.
Isa. 26:1 - In that day this song will be sung in the land of Judah: "We have a strong city; God will appoint salvation for walls and bulwarks."

Isa. 30:29 - You shall have a song As in the night when a holy festival is kept, And gladness of heart as when one goes with a flute, To come into the mountain of the Lord, To the Mighty One of Israel.

Isa. 42:10 - Sing to the Lord a new song, And His praise from the ends of the earth, You who go down to the sea, and all that is in it, You coastlands and you inhabitants of them!

SPEAK

Isa. 8:10 - Take counsel together, but it will come to nothing; Speak the word, but it will not stand, For God is with us.

Isa. 8:20 - To the law and to the testimony! If they do not speak according to this word, it is because there is no light in them.

Isa. 14:10 - They all shall speak and say to you: "Have you also become as weak as we? Have you become like us?"

Isa. 19:18 - In that day five cities in the land of Egypt will speak the language of Canaan and swear by the Lord of hosts; one will be called the City of Destruction.

Isa. 28:11 - For with stammering lips and another tongue He will speak to this people.

Isa. 29:4 - You shall be brought down, You shall speak out of the ground; Your speech shall be low, out of the dust; Your voice shall be like a medium's, out of the ground; And your speech shall whisper out of the dust.

Isa. 30:10 - Who say to the seers, "Do not see," And to the prophets, "Do not prophesy to us right things; Speak to us smooth things, prophesy deceits."

Isa. 32:4 - Also the heart of the rash will understand knowledge, And the tongue of the stammerers will be ready to speak plainly.

Isa. 32:6 - For the foolish person will speak foolishness, And his heart will work iniquity: To practice ungodliness, To utter error against the Lord, To keep the hungry unsatisfied, And he will cause the drink of the thirsty to fail.

Isa. 36:5 - I say you speak of having plans and power for war; but they are mere words. Now in whom do you trust, that you rebel against me?

Isa. 36:11 - Then Eliakim, Shebna, and Joah said to the Rabshakeh, "Please speak to your servants in the Aramaic language, for we understand it; and do not speak to us in Hebrew in the hearing of the people who are on the wall."

Isa. 36:12 - But the Rabshakeh said, "Has my master sent me to your master and to you to speak these words, and not to the men who sit on the wall, who will eat and drink their own waste with you?"

Isa. 37:10 - Thus you shall speak to Hezekiah king of Judah, saying: "Do not let your God in whom you trust deceive you, saying, Jerusalem shall not be given into the hand of the king of Assyria."

Isa. 40:2 - Speak comfort to Jerusalem, and cry out to her, That her warfare is ended, That her iniquity is pardoned; For she has received from the Lord's hand Double for all her sins.

Isa. 40:27 - Why do you say, O Jacob, And speak, O Israel: "My way is hidden from the Lord, And my just claim is passed over by my God"?

Isa. 41:1 - Keep silence before Me, O coastlands, And let the people renew their strength! Let them come near, then let them speak; Let us come near together for judgment.

Isa. 45:19 - I have not spoken in secret, In a dark place of the earth; I did not say to the seed of Jacob, 'Seek Me in vain'; I, the Lord, speak righteousness, I declare things that are right.

Isa. 50:4 - The Lord God has given Me The tongue of the learned, That I should know how to speak A word in season to him who is weary. He awakens Me morning by morning, He awakens My ear To hear as the learned.

Isa. 56:3 - Do not let the son of the foreigner Who has joined himself to the Lord Speak, saying, "The Lord has utterly separated me from His people"; Nor let the eunuch say, "Here I am, a dry tree."

Isa. 59:4 - No one calls for justice, Nor does any plead for truth. They trust in empty words and speak lies; They conceive evil and bring forth iniquity.

Isa. 63:1 - Who is this who comes from Edom, With dyed garments from Bozrah, This One who is glorious in His apparel, Traveling in the greatness of His strength? —"I who speak in righteousness, mighty to save."

SPEEDILY

Isa. 58:8 - Then your light shall break forth like the morning, Your healing shall spring forth speedily, And your righteousness shall go before you; The glory of the Lord shall be your rear guard.

SPIRIT

Isa. 4:4 - When the Lord has washed away the filth of the daughters of Zion, and purged the blood of Jerusalem from her midst, by the spirit of judgment and by the spirit of burning.

Isa. 11:2 - The Spirit of the Lord shall rest upon Him, The Spirit of wisdom and understanding, The Spirit of counsel and might, The Spirit of knowledge and of the fear of the Lord.

Isa. 19:3 - The spirit of Egypt will fail in its midst; I will destroy their counsel, And they will consult the idols and the charmers, The mediums and the sorcerers.

Isa. 19:14 - The Lord has mingled a perverse spirit in her midst; And they have caused Egypt to err in all her work, As a drunken man staggers in his vomit.

Isa. 26:9 - With my soul I have desired You in the night, Yes, by my spirit within me I will seek You early; For when Your judgments are in the earth, The inhabitants of the world will learn righteousness.

Isa. 28:6 - For a spirit of justice to him who sits in judgment, And for strength to those who turn back the battle at the gate.

Isa. 29:10 - For the Lord has poured out on you The spirit of deep sleep, And has closed your eyes, namely, the prophets; And He has covered your heads, namely, the seers.

Isa. 29:24 - These also who erred in spirit will come to understanding, And those who complained will learn doctrine.

Isa. 30:1 – "Woe to the rebellious children," says the Lord, "Who take counsel, but not of Me, And who devise plans, but not of My Spirit, That they may add sin to sin."

Isa. 31:3 - Now the Egyptians are men, and not God; And their horses are flesh, and not spirit. When the Lord stretches out His hand, Both he who helps will fall, And he who is helped will fall down; They all will perish together.

Isa. 32:15 - Until the Spirit is poured upon us from on high, And the wilderness becomes a fruitful field, And the fruitful field is counted as a forest.

Isa. 34:16 - Search from the book of the Lord, and read: Not one of these shall fail; Not one shall lack her mate.

For My mouth has commanded it, and His Spirit has gathered them.

Isa. 37:7 - Surely I will send a spirit upon him, and he shall hear a rumor and return to his own land; and I will cause him to fall by the sword in his own land.

Isa. 38:16 - O Lord, by these things men live; And in all these things is the life of my spirit; So You will restore me and make me live.

Isa. 40:13 - Who has directed the Spirit of the Lord, Or as His counselor has taught Him?

Isa. 42:1 - Behold! My Servant whom I uphold, My Elect One in whom My soul delights! I have put My Spirit upon Him; He will bring forth justice to the Gentiles.

Isa. 42:5 - Thus says God the Lord, Who created the heavens and stretched them out, Who spread forth the earth and that which comes from it, Who gives breath to the people on it, And spirit to those who walk on it.

Isa. 44:3 - For I will pour water on him who is thirsty, And floods on the dry ground; I will pour My Spirit on your descendants, And My blessing on your offspring.

Isa. 48:16 - Come near to Me, hear this: I have not spoken in secret from the beginning; From the time that it was, I was there. And now the Lord God and His Spirit Have sent Me.

Isa. 54:6 – "For the Lord has called you Like a woman forsaken and grieved in spirit, Like a youthful wife when you were refused," Says your God.

Isa. 57:15 - For thus says the High and Lofty One Who inhabits eternity, whose name is Holy: "I dwell in the high and holy place, With him who has a contrite and humble spirit, To revive the spirit of the humble, And to revive the heart of the contrite ones."

Isa. 57:16 - For I will not contend forever, Nor will I always be angry; For the spirit would fail before Me, And the souls which I have made.

Isa. 59:19 - So shall they fear The name of the Lord from the west, And His glory from the rising of the sun; When the enemy comes in like a flood, The Spirit of the Lord will lift up a standard against him.

Isa. 59:21 – "As for Me," says the Lord, "this is My covenant with them: My Spirit who is upon you, and My words which I have put in your mouth, shall not depart from your mouth, nor from the mouth of your descendants, nor from the mouth of your descendants' descendants," says the Lord, "from this time and forevermore."

Isa. 61:1 - The Spirit of the Lord God is upon Me, Because the Lord has anointed Me To preach good tidings to the poor; He has sent Me to heal the brokenhearted, To proclaim liberty to the captives, And the opening of the prison to those who are bound.

Isa. 61:3 - To console those who mourn in Zion, To give them beauty for ashes, The oil of joy for mourning, The garment of praise for the spirit of heaviness; That they may be called trees of righteousness, The planting of the Lord, that He may be glorified.

Isa. 63:10 - But they rebelled and grieved His Holy Spirit; So He turned Himself against them as an enemy, And He fought against them.

Isa. 63:11 - Then he remembered the days of old, Moses and his people, saying: "Where is He who brought them up out of the sea With the shepherd of His flock? Where is He who put His Holy Spirit within them."

Isa. 63:14 - As a beast goes down into the valley, And the Spirit of the Lord causes him to rest, So You lead Your people, To make Yourself a glorious name.

Isa. 65:14 - Behold, My servants shall sing for joy of heart, But you shall cry for sorrow of heart, And wail for grief of spirit.

Isa. 66:2 - "For all those things My hand has made, And all those things exist," Says the Lord. "But on this one will I look: On him who is poor and of a contrite spirit, And who trembles at My word."

STORE

Isa. 3:1 - For behold, the Lord, the Lord of hosts, Takes away from Jerusalem and from Judah The stock and the store, The whole supply of bread and the whole supply of water.

STRENGTH

Isa. 10:13 - For he says: "By the strength of my hand I have done it, And by my wisdom, for I am prudent; Also I have removed the boundaries of the people, And have robbed their treasuries; So I have put down the inhabitants like a valiant man."

Isa. 12:2 - Behold, God is my salvation, I will trust and not be afraid; 'For YAH, the Lord, is my strength and song; He also has become my salvation.

Isa. 23:4 - Be ashamed, O Sidon; For the sea has spoken, The strength of the sea, saying, "I do not labor, nor bring forth children; Neither do I rear young men, Nor bring up virgins."

Isa. 23:10 - Overflow through your land like the River, O daughter of Tarshish; There is no more strength.

Isa. 23:14 - Wail, you ships of Tarshish! For your strength is laid waste.

Isa. 25:4 - For You have been a strength to the poor, A strength to the needy in his distress, A refuge from the storm, A shade from the heat; For the blast of the terrible ones is as a storm against the wall.

Isa. 26:4 - Trust in the Lord forever, For in YAH, the Lord, is everlasting strength.

Isa. 27:5 - Or let him take hold of My strength, That he may make peace with Me; And he shall make peace with Me.

Isa. 28:6 - For a spirit of justice to him who sits in judgment, And for strength to those who turn back the battle at the gate.

Isa. 30:2 - Who walk to go down to Egypt, And have not asked My advice, To strengthen themselves in the strength of Pharaoh, And to trust in the shadow of Egypt!

Isa. 30:3 - Therefore the strength of Pharaoh Shall be your shame, And trust in the shadow of Egypt Shall be your humiliation.

Isa. 30:15 - For thus says the Lord God, the Holy One of Israel: "In returning and rest you shall be saved; In quietness and confidence shall be your strength. But you would not."

Isa. 33:6 - Wisdom and knowledge will be the stability of your times, And the strength of salvation; The fear of the Lord is His treasure.

Isa. 37:3 - And they said to him, "Thus says Hezekiah: 'This day is a day of trouble and rebuke and blasphemy; for the children have come to birth, but there is no strength to bring them forth.'"

Isa. 40:9 - O Zion, You who bring good tidings, Get up into the high mountain; O Jerusalem, You who bring good tidings, Lift up your voice with strength, Lift it up, be not afraid; Say to the cities of Judah, "Behold your God!"

Isa. 40:26 - Lift up your eyes on high, And see who has created these things, Who brings out their host by number; He calls them all by name, By the greatness of

His might And the strength of His power; Not one is missing.

Isa. 40:29 - He gives power to the weak, And to those who have no might He increases strength.

Isa. 40:31 - But those who wait on the Lord Shall renew their strength; They shall mount up with wings like eagles, They shall run and not be weary, They shall walk and not faint.

Isa. 41:1 - Keep silence before Me, O coastlands, And let the people renew their strength! Let them come near, then let them speak; Let us come near together for judgment.

Isa. 42:25 - Therefore He has poured on him the fury of His anger And the strength of battle; It has set him on fire all around, Yet he did not know; And it burned him, Yet he did not take it to heart.

Isa. 44:12 - The blacksmith with the tongs works one in the coals, Fashions it with hammers, And works it with the strength of his arms. Even so, he is hungry, and his strength fails; He drinks no water and is faint.

Isa. 45:24 - He shall say, 'Surely in the Lord I have righteousness and strength. To Him men shall come, And all shall be ashamed Who are incensed against Him.

Isa. 49:4 - Then I said, "I have labored in vain, I have spent my strength for nothing and in vain; Yet surely my just reward is with the Lord, And my work with my God."

Isa. 49:5 - And now the Lord says, Who formed Me from the womb to be His Servant, To bring Jacob back to Him, So that Israel is gathered to Him (For I shall be glorious in the eyes of the Lord, And My God shall be My strength)...

Isa. 51:9 - Awake, awake, put on strength, O arm of the Lord! Awake as in the ancient days, In the generations of old. Are You not the arm that cut Rahab apart, And wounded the serpent?

Isa. 52:1 - Awake, awake! Put on your strength, O Zion; Put on your beautiful garments, O Jerusalem, the holy city! For the uncircumcised and the unclean Shall no longer come to you.

Isa. 62:8 - The Lord has sworn by His right hand And by the arm of His strength: "Surely I will no longer give your grain As food for your enemies; And the sons of the foreigner shall not drink your new wine, For which you have labored."

Isa. 63:1 - Who is this who comes from Edom, With dyed garments from Bozrah, This One who is glorious in His apparel, Traveling in the greatness of His strength? —"I who speak in righteousness, mighty to save."

Isa. 63:6 - I have trodden down the peoples in My anger, Made them drunk in My fury, And brought down their strength to the earth.

Isa. 63:15 - Look down from heaven, And see from Your habitation, holy and glorious. Where are Your zeal and Your strength, The yearning of Your heart and Your mercies toward me? Are they restrained?

STUBBORN

Isa. 46:12 - Listen to Me, you stubborn-hearted, Who are far from righteousness.

STUMP

Isa. 6:13 - But yet a tenth will be in it, And will return and be for consuming, As a terebinth tree or as an oak, Whose stump remains when it is cut down. So the holy seed shall be its stump.

SWIFT
Isa. 18:2 - Which sends ambassadors by sea, Even in vessels of reed on the waters, saying, "Go, swift messengers, to a nation tall and smooth of skin, To a people terrible from their beginning onward, A nation powerful and treading down, Whose land the rivers divide."

Isa. 19:1 - The burden against Egypt. Behold, the Lord rides on a swift cloud, And will come into Egypt; The idols of Egypt will totter at His presence, And the heart of Egypt will melt in its midst.

Isa. 30:16 - And you said, "No, for we will flee on horses" —Therefore you shall flee! And, "We will ride on swift horses" —Therefore those who pursue you shall be swift!

SWIFTLY
Isa. 5:26 - He will lift up a banner to the nations from afar, And will whistle to them from the end of the earth; Surely they shall come with speed, swiftly.

TENDER
Isa. 47:1 - Come down and sit in the dust, O virgin daughter of Babylon; Sit on the ground without a throne, O daughter of the Chaldeans! For you shall no more be called Tender and delicate.

Isa. 53:2 - For He shall grow up before Him as a tender plant, And as a root out of dry ground. He has no form or comeliness; And when we see Him, There is no beauty that we should desire Him.

TENT
Isa. 38:12 - My life span is gone, Taken from me like a shepherd's tent; I have cut off my life like a weaver. He

cuts me off from the loom; From day until night You make an end of me.

Isa. 40:22 - It is He who sits above the circle of the earth, And its inhabitants are like grasshoppers, Who stretches out the heavens like a curtain, And spreads them out like a tent to dwell in.

Isa. 54:2 - Enlarge the place of your tent, And let them stretch out the curtains of your dwellings; Do not spare; Lengthen your cords, And strengthen your stakes.

THANKSGIVING

Isa. 51:3 - For the Lord will comfort Zion, He will comfort all her waste places; He will make her wilderness like Eden, And her desert like the garden of the Lord; Joy and gladness will be found in it, Thanksgiving and the voice of melody.

THORN

Isa. 55:13 - Instead of the thorn shall come up the cypress tree, And instead of the brier shall come up the myrtle tree; And it shall be to the Lord for a name, For an everlasting sign that shall not be cut off.

THRONE

Isa. 6:1 - In the year that King Uzziah died, I saw the Lord sitting on a throne, high and lifted up, and the train of His robe filled the temple.

Isa. 9:7 - Of the increase of His government and peace There will be no end, Upon the throne of David and over His kingdom, To order it and establish it with judgment and justice From that time forward, even forever. The zeal of the Lord of hosts will perform this.

Isa. 14:13 - For you have said in your heart: 'I will ascend into heaven, I will exalt my throne above the stars of God; I will also sit on the mount of the congregation On the farthest sides of the north.

Isa. 16:5 - In mercy the throne will be established; And One will sit on it in truth, in the tabernacle of David, Judging and seeking justice and hastening righteousness.

Isa. 22:23 - I will fasten him as a peg in a secure place, And he will become a glorious throne to his father's house.

Isa. 47:1 - Come down and sit in the dust, O virgin daughter of Babylon; Sit on the ground without a throne, O daughter of the Chaldeans! For you shall no more be called Tender and delicate.

Isa. 66:1 - Thus says the Lord: "Heaven is My throne, And earth is My footstool. Where is the house that you will build Me? And where is the place of My rest?"

TIDINGS

Isa. 40:9 - O Zion, You who bring good tidings, Get up into the high mountain; O Jerusalem, You who bring good tidings, Lift up your voice with strength, Lift it up, be not afraid; Say to the cities of Judah, "Behold your God!"

Isa. 41:27 - The first time I said to Zion, 'Look, there they are!' And I will give to Jerusalem one who brings good tidings.

Isa. 52:7 How beautiful upon the mountains Are the feet of him who brings good news, Who proclaims peace, Who brings glad tidings of good things, Who proclaims salvation, Who says to Zion, "Your God reigns!"

Isa. 61:1 - The Spirit of the Lord God is upon Me, Because the Lord has anointed Me To preach good tidings to the poor; He has sent Me to heal the brokenhearted, To proclaim liberty to the captives, And the opening of the prison to those who are bound.

TREMBLES
Isa. 66:2 – "For all those things My hand has made, And all those things exist," Says the Lord. "But on this one will I look: On him who is poor and of a contrite spirit, And who trembles at My word."

TRUST
Isa. 12:2 - Behold, God is my salvation, I will trust and not be afraid; "For YAH, the Lord, is my strength and song; He also has become my salvation."

Isa. 26:4 - Trust in the Lord forever, For in YAH, the Lord, is everlasting strength.

Isa. 30:2 - Who walk to go down to Egypt, And have not asked My advice, To strengthen themselves in the strength of Pharaoh, And to trust in the shadow of Egypt!

Isa. 30:3 - Therefore the strength of Pharaoh Shall be your shame, And trust in the shadow of Egypt Shall be your humiliation.

Isa. 30:12 - Therefore thus says the Holy One of Israel: "Because you despise this word, And trust in oppression and perversity, And rely on them."

Isa. 31:1 - Woe to those who go down to Egypt for help, And rely on horses, Who trust in chariots because they are many, And in horsemen because they are very strong, But who do not look to the Holy One of Israel, Nor seek the Lord!

Isa. 36:4 - Then the Rabshakeh said to them, "Say now to Hezekiah, 'Thus says the great king, the king of Assyria: "What confidence is this in which you trust?"

Isa. 36:5 - I say you speak of having plans and power for war; but they are mere words. Now in whom do you trust, that you rebel against me?

Isa. 36:6 - Look! You are trusting in the staff of this broken reed, Egypt, on which if a man leans, it will go into his hand and pierce it. So is Pharaoh king of Egypt to all who trust in him.

Isa. 36:7 - But if you say to me, "We trust in the Lord our God," is it not He whose high places and whose altars Hezekiah has taken away, and said to Judah and Jerusalem, "You shall worship before this altar'?"

Isa. 36:9 - How then will you repel one captain of the least of my master's servants, and put your trust in Egypt for chariots and horsemen?

Isa. 36:15 - Nor let Hezekiah make you trust in the Lord, saying, "The Lord will surely deliver us; this city will not be given into the hand of the king of Assyria."

Isa. 37:10 - Thus you shall speak to Hezekiah king of Judah, saying: "Do not let your God in whom you trust deceive you, saying, Jerusalem shall not be given into the hand of the king of Assyria."

Isa. 42:17 - They shall be turned back, They shall be greatly ashamed, Who trust in carved images, Who say to the molded images, "You are our gods."

Isa. 50:10 - Who among you fears the Lord? Who obeys the voice of His Servant? Who walks in darkness And has no light? Let him trust in the name of the Lord And rely upon his God.

Isa. 51:5 - My righteousness is near, My salvation has gone forth, And My arms will judge the peoples; The coastlands will wait upon Me, And on My arm they will trust.

Isa. 57:13 - When you cry out, Let your collection of idols deliver you. But the wind will carry them all away, A breath will take them. But he who puts his trust in Me shall possess the land, And shall inherit My holy mountain.

Isa. 59:4 - No one calls for justice, Nor does any plead for truth. They trust in empty words and speak lies; They conceive evil and bring forth iniquity.

UNCOVERED

Isa. 20:4 - So shall the king of Assyria lead away the Egyptians as prisoners and the Ethiopians as captives, young and old, naked and barefoot, with their buttocks uncovered, to the shame of Egypt.

Isa. 22:6 - Elam bore the quiver With chariots of men and horsemen, And Kir uncovered the shield.

Isa. 47:3 - Your nakedness shall be uncovered, Yes, your shame will be seen; I will take vengeance, And I will not arbitrate with a man.

Isa. 57:8 - Also behind the doors and their posts You have set up your remembrance; For you have uncovered yourself to those other than Me, And have gone up to them; You have enlarged your bed And made a covenant with them; You have loved their bed, Where you saw their nudity.

UNDONE

Isa. 6:5 - So I said: "Woe is me, for I am undone! Because I am a man of unclean lips, And I dwell in the midst of a people of unclean lips; For my eyes have seen the King, The Lord of hosts."

UPRIGHT

Isa. 26:7 - The way of the just is uprightness; O Most Upright, You weigh the path of the just.

VINEYARD

Isa. 1:8 - So the daughter of Zion is left as a booth in a vineyard, As a hut in a garden of cucumbers, As a besieged city.

Isa. 3:14 - The Lord will enter into judgment With the elders of His people And His princes: "For you have eaten up the vineyard; The plunder of the poor is in your houses."

Isa. 5:1 - Now let me sing to my Well-beloved A song of my Beloved regarding His vineyard: My Well-beloved has a vineyard On a very fruitful hill.

Isa. 5:3 - And now, O inhabitants of Jerusalem and men of Judah, Judge, please, between Me and My vineyard.

Isa. 5:4 - What more could have been done to My vineyard That I have not done in it? Why then, when I expected it to bring forth good grapes, Did it bring forth wild grapes?

Isa. 5:5 - And now, please let Me tell you what I will do to My vineyard: I will take away its hedge, and it shall be burned; And break down its wall, and it shall be trampled down.

Isa. 5:7 - For the vineyard of the Lord of hosts is the house of Israel, And the men of Judah are His pleasant plant. He looked for justice, but behold, oppression; For righteousness, but behold, a cry for help.

Isa. 5:10 - For ten acres of vineyard shall yield one bath, And a homer of seed shall yield one ephah.

Isa. 27:2 - In that day sing to her, "A vineyard of red wine!"

WARRIOR

Isa. 9:5 - For every warrior's sandal from the noisy battle, And garments rolled in blood, Will be used for burning and fuel of fire.

WORSHIP

Isa. 2:8 - Their land is also full of idols; They worship the work of their own hands, That which their own fingers have made.

Isa. 2:20 - In that day a man will cast away his idols of silver And his idols of gold, Which they made, each for himself to worship, To the moles and bats.

Isa. 27:13 - So it shall be in that day: The great trumpet will be blown; They will come, who are about to perish in the land of Assyria, And they who are outcasts in the land of Egypt, And shall worship the Lord in the holy mount at Jerusalem.

Isa. 36:7 - But if you say to me, "We trust in the Lord our God," is it not He whose high places and whose altars Hezekiah has taken away, and said to Judah and Jerusalem, "You shall worship before this altar?"

Isa. 46:6 - They lavish gold out of the bag, And weigh silver on the scales; They hire a goldsmith, and he makes it a god; They prostrate themselves, yes, they worship.

Isa. 49:7 - Thus says the Lord, The Redeemer of Israel, their Holy One, To Him whom man despises, To Him whom the nation abhors, To the Servant of rulers: "Kings shall see and arise, Princes also shall worship, Because of the Lord who is faithful, The Holy One of Israel; And He has chosen You."

Isa. 66:23 – "And it shall come to pass That from one New Moon to another, And from one Sabbath to another, All flesh shall come to worship before Me," says the Lord.

WRATH

Isa. 9:19 - Through the wrath of the Lord of hosts The land is burned up, And the people shall be as fuel for the fire; No man shall spare his brother.

Isa. 10:6 - I will send him against an ungodly nation, And against the people of My wrath I will give him charge, To seize the spoil, to take the prey, And to tread them down like the mire of the streets.

Isa. 13:9 - Behold, the day of the Lord comes, Cruel, with both wrath and fierce anger, To lay the land desolate; And He will destroy its sinners from it.

Isa. 13:13 - Therefore I will shake the heavens, And the earth will move out of her place, In the wrath of the Lord of hosts And in the day of His fierce anger.

Isa. 14:6 - He who struck the people in wrath with a continual stroke, He who ruled the nations in anger, Is persecuted and no one hinders.

Isa. 16:6 - We have heard of the pride of Moab—He is very proud—Of his haughtiness and his pride and his wrath; But his lies shall not be so.

Isa. 54:8 – "With a little wrath I hid My face from you for a moment; But with everlasting kindness I will have mercy on you," Says the Lord, your Redeemer.

Isa. 60:10 - The sons of foreigners shall build up your walls, And their kings shall minister to you; For in My wrath I struck you, But in My favor I have had mercy on you.

YOKE

Isa. 9:4 - For You have broken the yoke of his burden And the staff of his shoulder, The rod of his oppressor, As in the day of Midian.

Isa. 10:27 - It shall come to pass in that day That his burden will be taken away from your shoulder, And his yoke from your neck, And the yoke will be destroyed because of the anointing oil.

Isa. 14:25 - That I will break the Assyrian in My land, And on My mountains tread him underfoot. Then his yoke shall be removed from them, And his burden removed from their shoulders.

Isa. 47:6 - I was angry with My people; I have profaned My inheritance, And given them into your hand. You showed them no mercy; On the elderly you laid your yoke very heavily.

Isa. 58:6 - Is this not the fast that I have chosen: To loose the bonds of wickedness, To undo the heavy burdens, To let the oppressed go free, And that you break every yoke?

Isa. 58:9 - Then you shall call, and the Lord will answer; You shall cry, and He will say, "Here I am." If you take away the yoke from your midst, The pointing of the finger, and speaking wickedness.

TOPIC INDEX

153

MY OTHER PUBLICATIONS

To inquire about other books written by Eugene Carvalho, please visit the website below.

WWW.NEWWINEMISSIONS.INFO

<u>NOTES</u>

<u>NOTES</u>

<u>NOTES</u>

13839279R00084

Made in the USA
Charleston, SC
04 August 2012